The Ten Rules For Being Human

1. You will receive a body.
2. You will be presented with lessons.
3. There are no mistakes, only lessons.
4. Lessons are repeated until learned.
5. Learning does not end.
6. "There" is no better than "here."
7. Others are only mirrors of you.
8. What you make of your life is up to you.
9. All the answers lie inside of you.
10. You will forget all of this at birth.

IF LIFE IS A GAME, WHAT ARE THE RULES?

We all know the feeling: In the game of life, why am I the only one who doesn't know how to play? But now, help is at hand, because this wonderful little book will teach you the rules so that you can conquer life's challenges and manage its unpredictable ups and downs.

For one of her workshops several years ago, Chérie Carter-Scott, a corporate trainer and consultant, composed a list of basic truths about life, which she named "The Ten Rules for Being Human." Right away, the Rules resonated with her clients, who photocopied and passed the list to friends and relatives. Within months, Chérie's Rules were in thousands of homes all over the country, and eventually, they were published in CHICKEN SOUP FOR THE SOUL and have also appeared in Ann Landers' column. Although there's no formula to help you win the game of life, Chérie's Rules convey a universal wisdom that, once understood and embraced, can contribute to meaningful relationships with ourselves and others, at work and in the home.

In IF LIFE IS A GAME, THESE ARE THE RULES, Chérie shares that there are no mistakes in life, only lessons that are repeated. In thoughtful, inspirational essays illustrated with encouraging personal anecdotes, she includes the lessons that can be learned from each of the rules and offers insight on self-esteem, respect, acceptance, forgiveness, ethics, compassion, humility, gratitude, and courage. Best of all, Chérie shows that wisdom lies inside each one of us and that by putting the Ten Rules for Being Human into action we can create a more fulfilling life.

IF LIFE is
a GAME,
THESE are
the RULES

IF LIFE is a GAME, THESE are the RULES

Ten Rules for Being Human

as Introduced in

Chicken Soup for the Soul

CHÉRIE CARTER-SCOTT, PH.D.

Broadway Books   New York

IF LIFE IS A GAME, THESE ARE THE RULES. Copyright
© 1998 by Chérie Carter-Scott. All rights reserved. Printed in
the United States of America. No part of this book may be
reproduced or transmitted in any form or by any means,
electronic or mechanical, including photocopying, recording, or
by any information storage and retrieval system, without written
permission from the publisher. For information, address
Broadway Books, a division of Random House, Inc., 1540
Broadway, New York, NY 10036.

BROADWAY BOOKS titles may be purchased for business or
promotional use or for special sales. For information, please write
to: Special Markets Department, Random House, Inc., 1540
Broadway, New York, NY 10036.

BROADWAY BOOKS and its logo, a letter B bisected on the
diagonal, are trademarks of Broadway Books, a division of
Random House, Inc.

First export edition published 1999.

Chicken Soup for the Soul is a registered trademark.

Library of Congress Cataloging-in-Publication Data
    Carter-Scott, Chérie.
    If life is a game, these are the rules: ten rules for being
human, as introduced in Chicken soup for the soul / Chérie
Carter-Scott.—1st ed.
    p.   cm.
    ISBN 0-7679-0238-6 (hardcover)
    1. Conduct of life.   2. Spiritual life.   3. Success.
4. Chicken soup for the soul.   I. Title.
BJ1581.2.C256   1998
158.1—dc21   98-17458
CIP
Designed by Songhee Kim
Export Edition ISBN 0-7679-0388-9

99 98 99 00 01 02 03 10 9 8 7 6 5 4 3 2 1

If you came across the Rules for Being Human sometime during the last twenty-five years and photocopied them and passed them on to others; if you used the Rules for a retreat, class curriculum, brochure or Web site; if you framed the rules and put them on your wall, or tucked them in your drawer, or put them on the refrigerator door; if you read the Rules and smiled with recognition, then I dedicate this book to you and all seekers who have treasured the Rules for Being Human for these last twenty-five years. This book is to support you and those you love in your journey through Life. Use it as a primer for higher consciousness. Blessings to you on your path.

ACKNOWLEDGMENTS

Debra Goldstein has been my alter ego throughout the process of bringing this book into existence. She has been its guardian angel and essential to the quality of the finished product. Lauren Marino has been totally committed to these Rules becoming a spiritual primer for those on the path to higher consciousness. Trigg Robinson, Nancy Clare Morgan, and Donna Gould have been devoted to the world knowing the Rules are now explained in detail.

My loving, supportive, and dedicated partner, Lynn Stewart, who has helped me empower people through our workshops for over a quarter of a century; without her this book would not have been possible.

My devoted and loving husband, Michael A. Pomije, who supports me in all my wishes, hopes, and dreams.

My wonderful daughter, Jennifer Carter-Scott, who is my greatest teacher and toughest critic.

Jack Canfield, Mark Victor Hansen, and Patty

Aubery, who brought the Rules for Being Human into the light.

Michael Larsen and Elizabeth Pomada, who believed that this book had to be published.

To all those who have supported the evolutionary process of this book coming into existence: Barbara Adamich, Danita Allen, John Arno, Brook Ashley, Pam Beckerman, Nora Blanco, Jan Campbell, Jillian Dowling, Jenny Edwards, Connie Fueyo, Bob Furstenau, Penny A. Godlis, Carrell Halley, Katy Jacobson, Elena Johnston, Betty Mazetti Hatch, Richard Mantei, JoAnn Mermis, Greg Klein, Dan Millman, Terry Myrrdin, Molly Post, Joey Rosenberg, Jeri Rovsek, Julie Simpson, Linda Smukler, Helen Strodl, Marla Weiss, and Mady Widyasurya.

Barbara Rasmussen and Roger Hannegan, who celebrate this book from another place.

I am grateful for my friends, associates, family, and staff, who have all supported me.

CONTENTS

FOREWORD
by Jack Canfield

I have known Dr. Chérie Carter-Scott for over twenty years. I have taken her workshop, co-sponsored conferences with her, and had her consult with my organization, and she has been my own personal coach.

When we included the Rules for Being Human by "Anonymous" in *Chicken Soup for the Soul®*, I had no idea that Chérie was the author. When I learned that she was the author of the Rules, I was delighted yet not surprised. Chérie is a master facilitator whose life is dedicated to empowering and transforming people's experience of living life, so it made perfect sense that she would have created this astonishingly profound and simple template for understanding life.

While reading this book, you will begin to see your life from a whole new perspective. If you embrace the principles in this book, I promise you that your life will magically transform, and that you will learn the secrets to manifesting your heart's desire.

The Ten Rules for Being Human will open up many transformational opportunities for you. Enjoy the book, learn the lessons, and become a master of the game of life.

Jack Canfield
Co-author of *Chicken Soup for the Soul*®

PREFACE

In 1974, when I was twenty-five years old, I passed through a premature midlife crisis. I had pursued a career in teaching to please my mother, and then a career in acting to please myself. Neither one really satisfied me, and I was confused about what was next. The suggestions I received from family and friends only exacerbated the confusion. I didn't know where to turn for answers and so I started to pray for guidance.

After several weeks, I received three clear "messages"—from what divine source I was not really sure—that answered my questions. The first stated, "You are a catalyst for discovery." The second said, "You will work in growth and development." The third came through loud and clear, "You have a gift for working with people." I knew these three messages were the answer to my prayers, but I didn't know how to deploy them. These three "revelations" didn't point to an industry or provide me with a job description, so I was left trying to figure out what to do. I formulated a sentence: "I am a catalytic agent who works with people in their growth and development."

From that moment on, the messages came to me on a regular basis. They led me to create my seminar, the Inner Negotiation/Self-Esteem Workshop. In addition to the messages, people also started coming to me—to learn how to find their own inner answers. I started seeing people in one-to-one sessions to help them discover their own messages. Shortly thereafter, these same people requested a course in which they could quiet the voices of the mind and listen to their inner spirit. Subsequently, when I received requests from my clients, I responded by creating the programs they requested. People heard their inner directives, received answers to their questions, and, in turn, told their friends. And so my consulting business was launched, as well as a subsequent training program to teach other people how to do the same work I was doing.

One day, as I sat designing the training program for the Consultants Training, the Rules for Being Human came through me onto the paper. I thought, "I have been asking for these answers my whole life, and finally they have been delivered to me." The Rules answered the fundamental question I'd asked, "What is the purpose of life?" Delighted, I decided to include them as a handout in the three-month training course.

In the last twenty-four years, the Rules for Being

Human have circled the globe—photocopied and passed from friend to friend, transmitted via the Internet, printed on brochures and on page 81 in the book Jack Canfield wrote, *Chicken Soup for the Soul®*, where the Rules were attributed to "Anonymous." One day Jack called to say he'd heard from Dan Millman, the author of *The Way of the Peaceful Warrior*, that I was the author of the Rules for Being Human. Jack asked if that was true. When I acknowledged that I was, Jack apologized and offered to give me credit in the next printing.

Years have passed since that day. The most recent message that I have received was to write a book about the ten rules, so they can be passed on to everyone who is looking for a template for living a happy life. My hope is that this book will be a spiritual primer for those who are just setting out on their path, and a gentle reminder for those already well on their way.

Enjoy Ten Rules for Being Human, share them with others, use them to initiate conversations you have always wanted to have. Most of all, apply the Rules to your own life. Learn the lessons, listen to your messages, align with your spiritual DNA, and fulfill all your dreams.

Blessings on your journey,
Chérie Carter-Scott, Ph.D.

INTRODUCTION

"Life is a succession of lessons
which must be lived to be understood."

Helen Keller

Life has often been compared to a game. We are never told the rules, unfortunately, nor given any instructions about how to play. We simply begin at "Go" and make our way around the board, hoping we play it right. We don't exactly know the objective of playing, nor what it means to actually win.

That is what Ten Rules for Being Human is all about. These are the guidelines to playing the game we call life, but they are also much more than that. These Rules will provide you with a basic spiritual primer for what it means to be a human. They are universal truths that everyone inherently knows but has forgotten somewhere along the way. They form the foundation of how we can live a fulfilling, meaningful life.

Each Rule presents its own challenge, which in

turn provides certain lessons we all need to learn. Lessons are what you learn when you come up against problems that need to be solved and issues that need to be exorcised. Every person on the planet has his or her own set of lessons to learn that are separate and unique from everyone else's, and these lessons, as you will see in Rule Four, will reappear until they are mastered.

The Ten Rules for Being Human are not magic, nor do they promise ten easy steps to serenity. They offer no quick fix for emotional or spiritual ailments, and they are not fast-track secrets to enlightenment. Their only purpose is to give you a road map to follow as you travel your path of spiritual growth.

These Rules are not the oppressive rules and regulations that tell us what we should or should not do, or think, or say. These Rules are not mandates, but rather guidelines as to how to play the game. There is nothing you absolutely *must* do. I hope this book will help you to become more aware of them. By learning the valuable lessons and wisdom they offer, your journey on this Earth might just be a little bit easier.

YOU WILL RECEIVE A BODY

*You may love it or hate it, but it will be yours
for the duration of your life on Earth.*

The moment you arrived here on this Earth, you were given a body in which to house your spiritual essence. The real "you" is stored inside this body—all the hopes, dreams, fears, thoughts, expectations, and beliefs that make you the unique human that you are. Though you will travel through your entire lifetime together, you and your body will always remain two separate and distinct entities.

The purpose of this body is act as the buffer between you and the outside world and to transport you through this game we call life. It also acts as a teacher of some of the initial and fundamental lessons about being human. If you are open to all the lessons and gifts your body has to offer you, it can impart to you valuable bits of wisdom and grace that will guide you along your path of spiritual evolution. It can provide you with the basic knowledge and understanding you will need to be grounded within it before you can progress onward on your journey.

The body you are given will be yours for the duration of your time here. Love it or hate it, accept it or reject it, it is the only one you will receive in this lifetime. It will be with you from the moment you draw your first breath to the last beat of your heart. Since there is a no-refund, no-exchange policy on this body of yours, it is essential that you learn to transform your body from a mere vessel into a beloved partner and lifelong ally, as the relationship between you and your body is the most fundamental and important relationship of your lifetime. It is the blueprint from which all your other relationships will be built.

We each have a different relationship with our body. You may think of yours as a custom-designed home, ideally suited for your spirit and your soul. Or you may feel that your body is not well matched to your essence, thus trapping you in an ill-fitting cage. Perhaps you have a strong connection with your body, and you feel that you have an easy, satisfying, and familiar bond with it. You may be uncomfortable with your body and feel that you would like it to be different—stronger, thinner, healthier, more attractive, or less clumsy. Or perhaps you feel alienated from it, as if some mistake had been made when the body assignments were handed out. No matter what you may feel about your body, it is yours and the relationship you establish with it will have a great deal to do with the quality of your life experience.

The challenge of Rule One is to make peace with your body, so that it can effectively serve its purpose and share its valuable lessons of acceptance, self-esteem, respect, and pleasure. Everyone must learn these basic principles before he is able to journey successfully through life.

ACCEPTANCE

"I find that when we really love and accept and approve of ourselves exactly as we are, then everything in life works."

Louise Hay

If you are one of the rare and fortunate people who already experience your body as perfect exactly as it is, with all its foibles and strengths, then you have already embraced the lesson of acceptance and can fast-forward to the next lesson. However, if any small part of you believes that you would be happier if you were thinner, taller, larger, firmer, blonder, stronger, or some other physical alteration you think would magically transform your life for the better, then you might want to spend some time learning about the value of true acceptance.

Acceptance is the act of embracing what life presents to you with a good attitude. Our bodies are among the most willing and wise teachers of this lesson. Unless you spend a large percentage of your time engaged in out-of-body experiences, your body shows up wherever you are. It can be like an ever-present benevolent guide or a lifelong cross you bear. The decision is yours, based on how well you learn this lesson.

For many people, their body is the target for their harshest judgments and the barometer by which they measure their self-worth. They hold themselves up to an unattainable standard and berate themselves for coming up short of perfection. Since your physical shape is the form in which you show up in the world, it is very often the way you define yourself, and often the way others define you. The way you view your body is directly related to how close you are to learning the lesson of acceptance.

Imposing harsh judgments on your body limits the range of experiences you allow yourself to enjoy. How many times has a potentially wonderful day at the beach been tainted by your judgments about how you look in a bathing suit? Imagine how liberating it would be to happily walk across the warm sand without feeling self-conscious. Think of all the activities in your life that you have deferred until you look different, better, or perhaps even perfect. I have a friend who dreams of learning to scuba dive, but refuses to even try because she worries about how she would look swaddled in a tight rubber wet suit. Complete self-acceptance would allow her, and you, to fully participate in all aspects of life, without reservation, immediately.

Like many women I know, I spent years preoccupied with my thighs. I didn't just wish they were thinner, I was actually engaged in a private war with them. I wore the longest Bermuda shorts I could find, even on the hottest summer days, too embarrassed to expose them. I was convinced that my life would be enhanced if my thighs were firm and tight and didn't jiggle. I wanted my thighs to cooperate with my agenda of how I was supposed to look. I had disowned them, so of course, they reciprocated and stubbornly refused to magically transform themselves into taut, supple, wiry limbs. Suffice it to say, my thighs and I were not peacefully coexisting.

I finally decided to put an end to this cold war by vowing to learn to love my thighs. This was easier said than done. It is easy to love those parts of yourself that you already perceive as lovable, but far more difficult to give up your beliefs of how you should look. I decided to spend a few minutes every day giving positive attention to my perceived enemy. Every day I massaged rich vanilla-scented lotion into them. As I did this, I concentrated on sending them mental messages of partial then complete acceptance. For the first few weeks I felt ridiculous, but eventually I got over that. I still didn't look forward to seeing my thighs exposed in the harsh bathroom light every morning, but at least I didn't immediately cover them with a bath towel so as to conceal them from my own eyes.

As time passed, I actually did begin to appreciate my thighs for their strength and reliability. I gratefully acknowledged the support they give me, and their ability to sustain me on my daily three-mile run. Much to my delight, they responded in kind and began to cooperate by firming up. The key here, however, was not that they changed in order for me to accept them. It was because I accepted them that they eventually aligned with my wishes.

There is much documented proof that the mind and body are connected, so acceptance of your body is not only essential for your emotional well-being, it is essential for your physical health, as well. Denying your body complete acceptance can lead to illness, whereas practicing acceptance can heal disease. Even the modern medical community now embraces the value of self-acceptance for its power to maintain a healthy mind and body.

You know you are moving in the right direction when you can accept your body exactly as it is in its present form. True acceptance comes when you can embrace and appreciate your body as it is right now, and no longer feel that you need to alter it to be worthy of someone's love—most especially your own.

Does this mean that you should never endeavor to improve your body? Or that you have to be resigned to what you have been given? Of course not. It is perfectly natural and human to want to be at your physical best. What this does mean, however, is that you need to stop criticizing, judging, or finding fault with your body even when you are not at your healthiest or most attractive. The drive for self-improvement is completely healthy as long as it comes from a place of self-love rather than a feeling of inadequacy. The question to ask yourself when you want to be sure of the source of your desire for a new hairstyle or more sculpted biceps is, "Do I feel like I need this new body shape [or hair color, wrinkle cream, wardrobe—the list is long] to make me happy?" If the answer is yes—and be honest with yourself—you might want to spend some time working internally on the lesson of self-acceptance before you spend time and money searching for an external solution.

I frequently tell my clients and students, "Love all the parts of yourself, and if you can't love them, change them. If you can't change them, then accept them as they are." As you grow and age, your body will present you with some very challenging things that you simply cannot change. At the extreme end of the spectrum, you may be afflicted with a physical disability, or a debilitating disease, or some other physical ailment that makes your body that much harder to accept. But still accept it you must, no matter how insurmountable the task may seem. The Special Olympics are filled with people who have accepted their bodies despite obvious handicaps.

How can you begin to learn the lesson of acceptance? By recognizing that what is, just is, and that the key to unlocking the prison of self-judgment lies in your own mind. You can either continue to fight against your body's reality by complaining bitterly and immersing yourself in self-deprecation, or you can make the very subtle but powerful mental shift into acceptance. Either way, the reality remains the same. Acceptance or rejection of your body only carries weight in your mind; your perception has no bearing on how your body actually looks, so why not choose the ease of acceptance rather than the pain of rejection? The choice is yours.

What are you not accepting about your body?

SELF-ESTEEM

"No one can make you feel inferior without your consent."

Eleanor Roosevelt

Self-esteem is feeling worthy and able to meet life's challenges. It is as essential as the air we breathe, and just as intangible. It comes from the depths of our core, yet it is reflected in every single outward action we take, grand or small. It is the essence from which we measure our worth and the most important building block in the foundation of our psyches.

If self-esteem is a lesson that you need to learn, you will be tested over and over until you feel confident about who you are and understand and believe in your intrinsic value. Your body may provide you with enough opportunities to work on this lesson throughout your entire lifetime.

Your body may teach you the lesson of self-esteem by testing your willingness to view yourself as worthy, regardless of what you look like or how your body performs. A friend of mine is a public speaker who has had two major accidents in his life: first, a motorcycle accident set 90 percent of his body on fire, and then several years later, a small plane crash broke his back and put him in a wheelchair for the rest of his life. Through many years of hard inner work, he came to realize that in spite of his circumstances, he could live a fulfilled life as long as he approached it with the right attitude. Rather than dwelling on all the things he cannot do, he now focuses on those things he can do. His life's work is to inspire audiences with his lecture called "It's not what happens to you, it's what you do about it." He demonstrates on a daily basis that he is able to meet life's challenges and that he is worthy of happiness despite severe physical shortcomings.

The process of building self-esteem is threefold. The first step is to identify what stands in your way. By acknowledging the limiting belief that you have about yourself, you can then move to the second step: to search your soul for a deeper core connection with who you really are. The third step is to take action, whether that means valuing yourself just as you are or making a positive change.

Throughout her life, my dear friend Helen has been a strikingly attractive woman. She used to have gorgeous white-blond hair, which, when juxtaposed against her sun-bronzed skin, made heads turn when she entered a room. Helen's external identity was based on her arresting coloring, and so she maintained a deep tan year-round by spending many hours baking in the sun.

When Helen was in her late forties, she was diagnosed with skin cancer. She had to undergo surgery on her face, which left a small scar, and she was no longer permitted to sunbathe. To Helen, the scar was of minimal concern compared to the fact that she would no longer be the bronzed beauty she identified herself as. Without her trademark tan, Helen would have to dye her hair back to its original brown to avoid looking washed out. Helen's self-esteem plummeted as she struggled to accept the loss of what had been "her look" all those years. She needed to let go of the former image she had of herself.

It took Helen close to a year to repair her self-esteem. She needed to identify that she was measuring her worth by her external appearance, which had been that of a tanned blond. Through many months of hard work, she was able to reconnect with the core of who she is and realize that that belief was holding her back from feeling good about herself again.

It is now several years later, and Helen's scar is barely noticeable. She has returned to her natural coloring and now has lovely brown hair and ivory skin. Sometimes when she looks in the mirror, she needs to remind herself of her inherent worth by connecting to her inner source: her spiritual essence. She realizes that her true inner self will be with her for the rest of her life, while looks will change and fade—ultimately being an unreliable source of self-esteem.

Remind yourself often that self-esteem is ephemeral. You will have it, lose it, cultivate it, nurture it, and be forced to rebuild it over and over

again. It is not something to be achieved and pre-
served, but rather a lifelong process to be explored
and cultivated.

Where do your feelings of worthiness stem
from? Search to discover the pathway to that source,
for you will need to revisit that source again and
again throughout your lifetime. When you can easily
find your way to the core of your essential value,
then you know you have learned this lesson.

RESPECT

*"Your body is your vehicle for life. As long as you are here, live
in it. Love, honor, respect and cherish it, treat it well, and it
will serve you in kind."*

Suzy Prudden

To respect your body means to hold it in high regard
and honor it. Respect is treating your body with the
same care you would give any other valuable and
irreplaceable object. Learning to respect your body
is vital.

When you respect your body, you are in part-
nership with it. You become grounded in your
physical body and able to benefit from all it has to
offer you. Respect carries reciprocal energy. Your
body will honor you when you honor it. Treat your
body as a structure worthy of respect and it will
respond in kind. Abuse or ignore it and it will

break down in various ways until you learn the lesson of respect.

I know a man named Gordon who views his body as a sacred temple. Besides keeping it extraordinarily fit through regular exercise and sports, he maintains excellent health by always caring for it diligently. He eats only healthy foods, would never dream of going out in the cold improperly dressed, and generally treats his body as a valuable treasure. As a result of all the love he gives it, his body never fails him. He is almost always at optimum performance. His body is his beloved partner and ready to do whatever he needs it to do.

Of course, each person's body is different. It could be considered a big stretch for anyone else to maintain the level of attentiveness Gordon gives his body. Every person's body has a specific formula that works for it. It is your responsibility to become acquainted with your body's individual requirements. No one diet works for everyone, nor does any one sleep or exercise regimen. True respect comes from learning what your body needs to run at optimum performance, and then making the commitment to honoring those needs.

At the opposite end of the respect spectrum is Travis, a twenty-nine-year-old diabetic who refused to take his disease seriously. Travis is a wealthy, handsome jet-setter who loved living in the fast lane. He indulged often in vodka martinis, stayed out late frequently, ate red meat and rich, sugary desserts, and eventually became addicted to cocaine. Despite his doctor's warnings, Travis refused to change any of his unhealthy behaviors. He would not accept that his illness made his body's requirements different from those of his friends.

The downward spiral continued for months, peppered with severe bouts of illness, until one day Travis crashed. A friend found him collapsed on the bathroom floor and intervened, saving Travis's life. Travis's lesson of respect was learned at a painful price, but he finally moved through the denial, neglect, and abuse and learned to honor his body's specific needs and uniqueness.

As Travis illustrates, learning to respect your body is challenging in a world filled with excess and temptation. Going along with the group and indulging yourself is sometimes a lot easier than respecting your boundaries. Indulging yourself now and then is fine—in fact, at times it is even healthy—as long as you are not compromising your own special requirements. If you know spicy food makes you sick, but you love it anyway, how many times do you need to indulge and compromise your body's truth before you learn to respect its limitations? Not too many, I hope, for your own sake.

Treat your body with deference and respect, and it will respond accordingly. Listen to your body and its wisdom; it will tell you what it needs if you ask, listen, and take heed.

PLEASURE

"It ain't no sin to be glad you're alive."
Bruce Springsteen

Pleasure is the physical manifestation of joy. Your body teaches you pleasure through your five senses. When you indulge in any spontaneous behavior or physical sensation that unlocks the joy stored within you, you create space in your consciousness for pleasure.

Your body can be one of the greatest sources of pleasure when you open your five senses fully and experience the physical wonder of being alive. Pleasure can come in the form of sight, like when you see a magnificent sunset, or taste, like when you eat a favorite food. It can come as a glorious musical sound or the soft touch of a lover. The only secret to learning the lesson of pleasure is to make time and space for it in your life.

How much pleasure will you allow yourself? Many people have an invisible quota in their minds for the amount of joy they will permit themselves to experience. They become so busy living life that they view pleasure as a luxury they simply do not have time for. Things like lovemaking or playing take a backseat to the everyday motions of living.

However, your life simply will not work as well when you deny yourself pleasure. The old adage of all work and no play making you dull is quite true;

you may find yourself living a rather colorless life if you do not pause every now and then to indulge your senses. Pleasure is like the oil that keeps the machine of your life running smoothly. Without it, the gears stick and you will most likely break down.

Sometimes I forget the importance of pleasure as I race through the demands and commitments of my life. I forgo a day at the beach with my husband in order to finish a project, or I cancel my appointment for a massage so I can take care of errands. Inevitably, I begin to feel irritable and tense, which is a signal to me that I need to slow down and let in a little joy.

I had a man in one of my workshops named Bill who desperately needed to learn the lesson of pleasure. Bill was a very successful financial consultant at a large bank. He had a wife, three children, a mortgage, an elderly mother, two cars, and plenty of bills. Ordinarily a serious person, Bill had become practically austere in his demeanor as he grimly set about performing his tasks and managing his busy life. As he put it, he "simply did not have the time to waste on fun."

Yet Bill's life was not working. A deep dissatisfaction haunted him every day, and he didn't know how to dislodge it. He came to the workshop to figure out how to change the grind he had put himself into. In the workshop, he realized that he had not allowed himself a single moment of pleasure in many years. Bill remembered the day when his father died, when little Billy was only eleven years old. His uncle told him that he would have to step in as the man of the family. On that day, Billy metamorphosed from a carefree child to Bill, a mature, responsible little adult.

When we did an exercise in the workshop in which everyone was to act upon an inner impulse, Bill stood up, loosened his tie, and much to everyone's surprise and delight, began to skip around the room. He started slowly, then skipped faster and faster, until he was whizzing by us in a blur. When he finally came to a stop, he was breathless and smiling, obviously thrilled to have unlocked the joy stored in his cellular memory.

What brings you pleasure? Do it, and do it often, for it will give lightness to your heart and do wonders for your soul.

Rule Two

YOU WILL BE PRESENTED WITH LESSONS

You are enrolled in a full-time informal school called "life." Each day in this school you will have the opportunity to learn lessons. You may like the lessons or hate them, but you have designed them as part of your curriculum.

Why are you here? What is your purpose? Humans have sought to discover the meaning of life for a very long time. What we and our ancestors have overlooked, however, in the course of this endless search, is that there is no *one* answer. The meaning of life is different for every individual.

Each person has his or her own purpose and distinct path, unique and separate from anyone else's. As you travel your life path, you will be presented with numerous lessons that you will need to learn in order to fulfill that purpose. The lessons you are presented with are specific to you; learning these lessons is the key to discovering and fulfilling the meaning and relevance of your own life.

Once you have learned the basic lessons taught to you by your own body, you are ready for a more advanced teacher: the universe. You will be presented with lessons in every circumstance that surfaces in your life. When you experience pain, you learn a lesson. When you feel joy, you learn a different lesson. For every action or event, there is an accompanying lesson that must be learned. There really is no way to avoid the lessons you are presented with, nor is there any chance that you will be able to skirt around the learning process.

As you travel through your lifetime, you may encounter challenging lessons that others don't have to face, while others spend years struggling with challenges that you don't need to deal with. You may never know why you are blessed with a wonderful marriage, while your friends suffer through bitter arguments and painful divorces, just as you cannot be sure why you struggle financially while your peers enjoy abundance. The only thing you can count on for certain is that you will be presented with *all* the lessons that you specifically need to learn; whether you choose to learn them or not is entirely up to you.

The challenge of Rule Two, therefore, is to align yourself with your own unique path by learning your individual lessons. This is one of the most difficult challenges you will be faced with in your lifetime, as sometimes your path will lead you into a life that is radically different from others'. Don't compare your path to those of the people around you and focus on the disparity between their lessons and yours. You need to remember that you will only be faced with lessons that you are capable of learning and are specific to your own growth.

If you are able to rise to this challenge, you can unravel the mystery of your purpose and actually live it. You cease being a victim of fate or circumstances and become empowered—life no longer just "happens to you." When you are working toward fulfilling your true purpose you discover astonishing gifts within yourself that you may have never known you have. This process may not be easy, but the rewards are well worth the struggle.

As you strive to discover and learn about yourself, you will most likely encounter the basic lessons of openness, choice, fairness, and grace. Look at these lessons as tools to help you discover your own unique purpose.

OPENNESS

"When experience is viewed in a certain way, it presents nothing but doorways into the domain of the soul."

Jon Kabat-Zinn

Openness means being receptive. Life will present you with innumerable lessons, none of which will be useful to you unless you recognize them and are open to their inherent value. These lessons will show up every day of your life, and as difficult as some of them may be you need to change your perception and come to see them as gifts, or guides along your path toward living as your authentic self.

I have watched hundreds of people in my workshops experience the profound transformation that comes when they understand that every event in their lives occurs to teach them something about themselves. When you accept the lessons that life brings you, no matter how unpleasant or challenging they may be, you take the crucial first step toward finding your true self and your purpose. You begin to cultivate the essential attitude of openness.

I am often asked how people can recognize their lessons. My response is that each person's lessons are always self-evident; it is just a matter of what lenses the person is wearing at the time. If they are wearing the lenses of resistance, they may become angry or bitter and this stubbornness will prevent their per-

sonal growth. If they are wearing the lenses of openness and clear discernment, they will gain a deeper
understanding of what different life situations can
teach them.

It is easy to spot those lessons that you perceive
as opportunities, because they are attractive. Getting
a big promotion at work does present certain
lessons, such as responsibility and willingness. Em-
barking on a new love affair presents some lessons,
like trust and compromise. Becoming a parent for
the first time teaches the lessons of patience and dis-
cipline. These lessons are easily recognized because
they come wrapped in attractive packages. Being
open to these lessons isn't so hard.

More difficult to recognize are the lessons that
make it seem as though you are getting a raw deal
from life. These lessons come wrapped in less attractive packages and tend to cause most people to
quickly put on their resistance lenses. When you are
not open to seeing your lessons, losing your job
looks like a catastrophe rather than an opportunity
to learn the lessons of forgiveness or flexibility.
Experiencing heartbreak can look like a crisis, rather
than a hint to learn the lessons of kindness or unattachment. Becoming a parent for the first time to a
child who is disabled can appear to be punishment,
rather than a chance to learn about healing or support. While the less attractive lessons may not be
fun, they can actually be the biggest gifts you receive.

For me, the lesson that came up recently is patience. I knew it was a lesson I needed to learn because I constantly found myself in situations in which I felt rushed, irritated, and annoyed. I needed to learn this one, but every time it presented itself, I seemed to get those resistance glasses on before I was able to see the opportunity to work it out. I was convinced that *this* particular situation was one in which I really, really needed to get things done my way quickly, and that my resulting frustration had absolutely nothing to do with my needing to learn the lesson of patience. The lesson was camouflaged by my resistance.

How can we move from resistance to openness? By first recognizing the feeling of resistance. Resistance usually manifests itself physically in a clenched jaw, a tightness in the chest, or sighing. Mentally, it shows up in thoughts like, "Why do I have to deal with this issue? I don't want this, I don't need it, I don't like it!" Once you discover where in your mind or body resistance anchors itself, you can more easily identify it in the future.

The next step is to remind yourself that you have a choice. You can either continue with this resistance and feel badly or you can learn whatever the lesson is there to teach you. Presenting yourself with a choice allows you to see that you have control over your resistance and how you choose to deal with life's challenges.

The last step is to ask yourself, "Am I willing to give up the resistance and learn whatever lesson is presenting itself?" Remember, if you want to truly live from your authentic self, you must be open to learning all the lessons you are given so that you may grow into the person you want to become.

What lessons are you resisting?

CHOICE

"I will do strongly before the sun and moon whatever inly rejoices me and the heart appoints."

Ralph Waldo Emerson

Choice is the exploration of desire and then the selection of action. In every moment, you are choosing either to align yourself with your own true path or to veer away from it. There are no neutral actions. Even the smallest gesture has a direction to it, leading you closer to your path or farther away from it, whether you realize it or not. Pure actions—like spending time with a beloved friend—bring you into alignment, whereas false ones—such as spending time with someone you *really* don't like but to whom you feel obligated—alienate you from your truth. Every choice carries weight.

Though used synonymously, choice and decision are not the same thing. Decisions are made in your mind, whereas choices are made in your gut. Deci-

IF LIFE IS A GAME,THESE ARE THE RULES
978076790388   5.85
COLORECTAL CANCER
09012901495   13.45

TOTAL $ 18.30
CASH $ 20.00
CHANGE $ 0.70

ITEMS 2
12/17/1999 20:09   3160 29 000516 1295

ADJUSTMENTS MADE WITHIN
90 DAYS FOR ALL OTHER ITEMS

SAVE YOUR RECEIPT

ADJUSTMENTS MADE WITHIN 30
DAYS FOR WATCHES, JEWELRY
ELECTRONICS, COMPUTERS,
UNOPENED PRERECORDED
MUSIC, VIDEO GAMES AND
SOFTWARE.

ADJUSTMENTS MADE WITHIN
90 DAYS FOR ALL OTHER ITEMS

SAVE YOUR RECEIPT

ADJUSTMENTS MADE WITHIN 30
DAYS FOR WATCHES, JEWELRY
ELECTRONICS, COMPUTERS,
UNOPENED PRERECORDED
MUSIC, VIDEO GAMES AND
SOFTWARE.

ADJUSTMENTS MADE WITHIN
90 DAYS FOR ALL OTHER ITEMS

sions come from the rational, reasonable weighing of the circumstances; choices come from your essence and an attunement with your higher self.

Take, for example, an opera singer named Betty who needed to find a new career because her vocal cords were damaged. She came to me for consultation, unsure that she had any skills that would be useful in finding a new career. I assured Betty that she had some preferences and passions that would guide her, and asked her to tell me what it was she loved to do.

Betty thought for a while, and then acknowledged the four things she loved above all others: eating, shopping, speaking French, and dining in elegant restaurants. She practically lit up as she described her delight for each of these activities. Then Betty quickly added that she was aware that other people would not view these interests as valuable, and that she was sure they would do her no good in finding her new career.

However, that was where Betty was mistaken. By choosing to acknowledge and honor her real interests, she was able to take real steps that enabled her to align with her truth, rather than deciding to find a "reasonable" job that might lead her away from it. Betty chose to find a job that accommodated at least some of these interests.

Much to Betty's astonishment, she manifested a job that actually accommodated all of these seemingly disparate interests. She became a special events coordinator for a major upscale department store. Her first assignment was to entertain the executives from a couture French design company by dining with them in elegant restaurants.

Think back to an authentic choice you made at some point in your life. Perhaps it was a strong pull to visit a foreign country, or a feeling that a certain romantic relationship needed to end, or the sense that you needed to leave your corporate job and start your own business. How did it feel to act on your choices?

Remember that feeling. It is the essence of living aligned with your path.

FAIRNESS

"I cried because I had no shoes until I saw a man who had no feet."

Author Unknown

Our sense of fairness is the expectation of equity— the assumption that all things are equal and that justice will always prevail. Life is not, in fact, fair, and you may indeed have a more difficult life path than others around you, deserved or not. Everyone's circumstances are unique, and everyone needs to handle his or her own circumstances differently. As you work toward aligning yourself with your own individual truth, you will be required to move out of the complaining phase of "it's not fair," if you want to move toward serenity. Focusing on the unfairness of circumstances keeps you comparing yourself with others rather than appreciating your own special uniqueness. You miss out on learning your individual lessons by distracting yourself with feelings of bitterness and resentment.

Take, for example, Jackie and Kirsten, two sisters who are miles apart on the traditional beauty scale. Jackie was a tall, statuesque brunette with startling blue eyes, a graceful demeanor, and an elegant sense of style. She was so striking that people on the street would often stare as she passed by, certain that she was a movie star.

Kirsten, on the other hand, fit the classic definition of a tomboy. She was compact and plain-looking and rarely bothered with fashion or makeup. No one would ever mistake Kirsten for a movie star.

Jackie had been married twice, Kirsten never. Jackie always had men calling to ask for dates; Kirsten, far less frequently. Though no one would expect it judging from Kirsten's tough exterior, she spent a lot of her time comparing herself to her older sister, trapped in Jackie's shadow. She belabored the unfairness of the allotment of genes between Jackie and herself.

It was not until Kirsten finally sat down to make a list of all the things she was good at, and all the things that made her special, that she was able to see her own unique gifts and cease dwelling on the comparison with Jackie. She realized that her natural athletic ability was a true talent in which she could revel and excel, and that she had a gift for supporting those around her. Even though she acknowledged she would probably never turn heads the way Jackie did, she admitted many things she appreciated about her physical form and was delighted to see the list was quite long. Kirsten's lesson was to learn that just because she perceived something as unfair did not mean she had to wallow in the apparent injustice of it.

What perception of unfairness holds you back?

GRACE

"You nourish your soul by fulfilling your destiny."

Harold Kushner

Grace is one of those intangible qualities that is difficult to describe but easy to recognize. Those who possess grace seem to walk effortlessly through life. They give the illusion of glowing from within and that glow is apparent to everyone around them.

To live in a state of grace means to be fully in tune with your spiritual nature and a higher power that sustains you. Grace comes when you are able to move from your lower self, where your ego dictates the path that "should be" rightfully yours, to your higher self, where you are able to transcend your ego and expand into your greater good. It comes when you shift from a "me"-centered reality to an understanding of the bigger picture. Grace comes when you understand and accept that the universe always creates circumstances that lead every person to his or her own true path, and that everything happens for a reason as part of a divine plan.

Sounds wonderful, you might say, but how do you achieve such a blissful state? By remembering each and every day that the lessons you are presented with are special gifts uniquely for you, and that learning these lessons is what will bring you to a state of grace. By anchoring yourself in the belief that you will be given whatever is right for you, regardless of how far off it may be from your perceived personal agenda.

Take, for example, Delia, a young woman with a natural gift for writing. Delia came from a wealthy East Coast family, whose mandate for her was to get married to an equally wealthy man, move to a large house in the suburbs, and pursue some "appropriate" avocation like volunteering or fund-raising for a charity. However, Delia knew deep in her heart that her passion for writing was a divine gift, and that her true path was that of a writer. Naturally, her family was horrified when she announced she planned to move to New York and pursue a freelance writing career.

Delia eventually did pursue her dream. She loved

her small apartment downtown, met other aspiring writers with whom she could share her writing, and work came her way almost effortlessly. Her life felt as though it was flowing beautifully. Though she needed to deal with the disappointment of her family and the frightening reality of stepping out of the comfortable framework built for her, she stayed aligned with her truth. When I last saw Delia, she had been commissioned to write a long piece for a major magazine and possessed that inner glow of grace.

In the state of grace you trust in yourself and the universe. You can celebrate other people's blessings, knowing that their gifts are right and appropriate for them and that the universe has your gift right around the corner.

THERE ARE NO MISTAKES, ONLY LESSONS

Growth is a process of experimentation, a series of trials, errors, and occasional victories. The failed experiments are as much a part of the process as the experiments that work.

Human growth is a process of experimentation, trial, and error, ultimately leading to wisdom. Each time you choose to trust yourself and take action, you can never quite be certain how the situation will turn out. Sometimes you are victorious, and sometimes you become disillusioned. The failed experiments, however, are no less valuable than the experiments that ultimately prove successful; in fact, you usually learn more from your perceived "failures" than you do from your perceived "successes."

Most people feel great disappointment and anger when their plans in which they've invested a great deal of energy, time, and money fall through. The first reaction for most of us is to feel that we have failed. While it is easy enough to jump to this depressing conclusion, it will impede your ability to progress with your life lessons.

Rather than viewing your own mistakes as failures and others' mistakes as slights, you can view them as opportunities to learn. As Emerson said, "Every calamity is a spur and a valuable hint." Every situation in which you do not live up to your own expectations is an opportunity to learn something important about your own thoughts and behaviors. Every situation in which you feel "wronged" by another person is a chance to learn something about your reactions. Whether it is your own wrongdoing or someone else's, a mistake is simply an opportunity to evolve further along your spiritual path.

When you consider the hardships of life—the disappointments, hurts, losses, illnesses, all the tragedies you may suffer—and shift your perception to see them as opportunities for learning and growth, you become empowered. You can take charge of your life and rise to its challenges, instead of feeling defeated, victimized, or cast adrift.

A wonderful story that illustrates this is from *The Speed of Light*, by Gwyneth Cravens:

Asad told her story. It was about a young girl from Morocco whose father was a spinner. He became prosperous in his craft, and took her with him on a voyage in the Mediterranean. He wanted to sell his thread, and told his daughter that she should also look for a young man who would make her a good husband. But a storm caused the ship to flounder near Egypt, killing the father and casting the daughter ashore. Miserable and exhausted, barely able to remember her previous life, the girl wandered in the sand until she finally met a family of weavers. They took her in and taught her how to make cloth. Eventually she became contented.

But after a few years, she was captured on the seashore by slavers who then sailed East to Istanbul and took her to its slave market. A man who made ships' masts went to the market to buy slaves to help him with his work, but when he noticed the girl, he took pity on her, bought her, and took her home to serve his wife. But pirates stole the cargo he invested in, and he was unable to buy the other slaves. He, the girl, and his wife had to make all the masts themselves. The girl worked hard and con- scientiously. The mast maker found her to be so capable that he eventually granted her freedom and made her a partner in his business, which she came to enjoy.

One day he asked her to accompany a ship- ment of masts to Java. She agreed, but off the coast of China the ship was struck by a typhoon. Again she was washed up on a strange seashore, and again she cried out against fate. "Why do these bad things keep happening to me?" she asked. No answer came. She got up out of the sand and started walking inland.

There was a legend in China that a foreign woman would appear and make a tent for the emperor. Because nobody in China knew how to make tents, the whole population, including one generation of emperors after another, wondered about this prediction. Once a year, the emperor sent out emissaries to every town to bring all the foreign women to the royal court.

In due course, the shipwrecked woman arrived before the emperor, who asked her through an interpreter if she could make a tent. "I think I can," she said. She asked for rope, but the Chinese had none, and so, recalling her girlhood as the daughter of a spinner, she asked for silk and spun it into rope. She asked for thick cloth, but the Chinese had none, and so, recalling her life among the weavers, she wove the kind of cloth used for tents. She asked for tent poles, but the Chinese had none, and so, recalling her life with the mast maker, she made tent poles. When she had all these things ready, she tried to remember as best she could all the tents she had seen in her life. At last she put together a tent. The emperor marveled at the construction, and at the fulfillment of the old prophecy, and offered whatever she wished. She married a handsome prince, remained in China surrounded by her children, and lived to a happy old age. And she realized that although her adventures had seemed terrible when they were happening, they turned out to be essential for her ultimate happiness.

The girl in Asad's story saw, in hindsight, the magic within her dreadful circumstances. She was able to see the perfection in the grand scheme of things. While it is not always easy for us to view our situations from a macro-perspective, it is essential in order to find the good in what appears to be unfortunate circumstances.

To ease this process of learning, you must first master the basic lessons of compassion, forgiveness, ethics, and, ultimately, humor. Without these essential lessons, you remain trapped in your limited view and unable to parlay mistakes into valuable learning opportunities.

COMPASSION

"The individual is capable of both great compassion and great indifference. He has it within his means to nourish the former and outgrow the latter."

Norman Cousins

Compassion is the act of opening your heart. To live in a state of compassion means you approach the world with your emotional barriers lowered and your ability to connect with others intact. Compassion is the emotional glue that keeps you rooted in the universality of the human experience, as it connects you to your essence and to the essence of those around you.

We do not all walk around with our hearts wide open all the time, however; doing so would leave us overwhelmed and in emotional danger. If I kept my heart open and exposed while watching the six o'clock news every night, I would most likely never recover from the rush of helpless and hopeless feelings created by all the tragic stories. Sometimes it is necessary to keep your emotional barriers up as a way to protect yourself.

The key to learning the lesson of compassion is realizing that you are in control of the erection or destruction of those barriers that create distance between you and others. You can choose to dissolve those barriers when you want to connect with the heart of another human being. You can also choose to limit others' access to your heart when you need to, by forming judgments that separate you from that which you are judging.

Judgments are not always negative. Your judgments are what keep you from walking around like an open membrane, open and exposed to whatever information you come in contact with. At times, your judgments serve to help you decide what beliefs and thoughts you choose to let in from the outside world and help you discern what is true for you. Without your sense of judgment, you would be bombarded with hundreds of conflicting ideas over which you would have no power to discriminate.

At other times, however, your judgments can limit you and prevent you from being compassionate when and where that is needed. When your judgments become more overpowering than your ability to practice empathy, you separate yourself from your own human essence. You put yourself into a box of self-righteousness and seal yourself off from your innate need to connect with other people. You may feel superior to those you are judging, but you may also feel the chill of loneliness imposed by your isolation. The only antidote to rigid judgments is compassion.

The secret to learning to open your heart is the willingness to connect to your essence and the essence of the person you are judging. From there, the magic of compassion opens limitless doors to human connection.

In order to learn the lesson of compassion, you will first need to recognize when you have become trapped by your limiting judgments. The best way to do this is to pay attention to your breathing. If your breathing feels shallow or tight, you are most likely trapped in a judgment that needs to be released. Your conscious mind can also help identify when compassion is called for. Chances are, if you are able to pause in the middle of making a judgment long enough to consider compassion, then compassion is required. You would not have entertained the thought otherwise.

As you learned in Rule Two, you have the ability to choose whether or not you will learn the lessons you are presented with, so you will then need to use your discretion to choose whether to invite in compassion or remain closed. If you choose compassion, then you need to move the judgment from its position in your mind down into the emotional realm of your heart. It is there that you can try on what it would feel like to be that person you are judging and imagine putting yourself in her reality. This will connect you to her essence and evaporate the judgment encrusted around your heart.

A story that my friend Nicki told me about how she learned the lesson of compassion is one of the most powerful examples of human kindness I have ever heard. As a child, Nicki and her friend were molested on their way home from school by a man in a brown car. Nicki memorized the license plate of that brown car and told the police, who captured the offender and arrested him. Nicki remained deeply troubled by that incident for many years.

As an adult, Nicki became a social worker. She never quite forgot that episode from her childhood, and so she had a particular softness for victims of child abuse and molestation. One day, she was given the case of a sex offender who needed rehabilitation. Much to Nicki's horror, it was the man in the brown car, still committing these acts fifteen years later.

Nicki's mind immediately flooded with judgments. She recalled the shame and anger she felt all those years ago, and something close to hatred toward this man rose up in her. She still had difficulty believing that anyone could commit such a heinous act. She had no intention of doing anything to help the man who was responsible for her terrible memories.

In the midst of her judgments, Nicki realized one important fact: that this man was deeply troubled and needed to be helped. Though it was one of the most difficult decisions she ever made, Nicki chose to allow her heart to open to this man and assist him with his recovery. She got in touch with the part of her that knew that everyone, including herself, was capable of committing inappropriate acts at times. By connecting to her essence, she allowed herself to imagine the pain this man must have been in that caused him to behave the way he did; it was by imagining herself in his reality that she was able to release her judgments and move into compassion.

Compassion is also required at those times when you are harshly judging yourself. If you have made what you perceive to be a mistake, behaved in some way of which you are not proud, or failed to live up to your own expectations, you will most likely put up a barrier between your essence and the part of you that is the alleged wrongdoer. By doing this, you create a chasm wide enough to hold some severely self-critical thoughts. Such a barrier is no less restrictive or destructive than one that divides you from other people.

At those times, you will need to consciously open your heart to yourself and show compassion. Compassion will then open the door to the possibility of forgiveness and will allow you to release those judgments that are holding you in self-contempt.

What judgments do you need to transcend to learn the lesson of compassion?

FORGIVENESS

"To err is human, to forgive, divine."

Alexander Pope

Forgiveness is the act of erasing an emotional debt. As you move from compassion to forgiveness, your heart is already open, and you engage in a conscious and deliberate release of resentment. Perceiving past actions as mistakes implies guilt and blame, and it is not possible to learn anything meaningful while you are engaged in blaming.

There are four kinds of forgiveness. The first is beginner forgiveness for yourself. Not long ago, I got lost on the New York subway. I was late for a meeting with a friend, causing her to wait for me in the freezing rain for nearly an hour. I felt absolutely terrible, and was on the verge of beating myself up, when I boarded yet another train to try to reach my destination. I finally realized that I was doing the very best I could under the circumstances. I remembered the value of extending compassion toward myself and made amends by sincerely apologizing when I reached my friend. I then released the situation.

The second kind of forgiveness is beginner forgiveness for another. This is where you need to forgive someone for a moderate transgression. For instance, my friend who had to wait for me in the rain could have been really upset and held a grudge; but instead of harboring resentment, she graciously accepted my apology and we repaired the temporary rift. When I asked her to tell me how she forgave me so quickly, she said she knew I didn't intend to make her wait. She herself had been lost in the subway in the past, and identified with my situation. Though she was initially annoyed, she recognized that staying angry would only waste her energy and cause me more guilt. She chose to forgive me instead.

You may resist learning this lesson because sometimes it feels *good* to blame people for their mistakes. It makes you feel superior and righteous when you can look down your nose and hold a grudge toward someone who has wronged you. However, harboring resentments consumes a lot of energy. Why waste valuable energy on prolonged anger and guilt, when you could use that energy for far greater things? When you let go of resentment, guilt, and anger, you become revitalized and create space in your soul for growth.

The third kind of forgiveness is advanced forgiveness of yourself. This is for serious transgressions, the ones you carry with deep shame. When you do something that violates your own values and ethics, you create a chasm between your standards and your actual behavior, which compromises your integrity. You need to work very hard at forgiving yourself for these deeds so that you can close this chasm and realign with the best part of yourself. I am not saying that you should drown out the voice of your conscience by rushing to forgive yourself or not feeling regret or remorse; but wallowing in these feelings for a protracted period of time is not healthy. Continuing to punish yourself only creates a bigger gap between you and your ethics, and the bigger that gap, the greater the chance that you will repeat the unacceptable behavior. Remember, your conscience is not your enemy; it is there to remind you to stay on track and stick to your values. Just notice the feeling it is sending you, learn the lesson, and move on.

The last and perhaps most difficult kind of forgiveness is the advanced forgiveness of another. Everyone I know has been morally wronged or severely hurt by another person at some time in his or her life to such a degree that forgiveness seems impossible. However, harboring resentment and revenge fantasies only keeps you trapped in victimhood. It is only through forgiveness that you can erase wrongdoing and clean the slate.

At the age of forty-five, a woman named Margo was abandoned by her husband. After twelve years of marriage, he emptied their bank account and safe deposit box and took off with another woman. Besides being emotionally devastated, Margo was terrified, since she had no career training and no means of supporting herself. She felt a loathing toward her husband of which she had never imagined she was capable.

It took Margo three years to get her life back on track. She borrowed money from her sister to go back to school to get a mortgage broker's license, and eventually she started her own business. Margo now feels a sense of real accomplishment, since the business is thriving. Though she still feels sad about the loss of her husband, she no longer carries around the intense hatred that controlled her for so long.

Margo was finally able to forgive her husband when she shifted out of victimhood and forced herself to see the bigger picture. She was able to shift the focus away from her anger onto seeing the opportunity for growth in the present situation. In hindsight, she can finally view the entire event as a valuable learning experience; after all, without this apparent tragedy, she might never have come into her own power and learned advanced forgiveness.

So, again, here are the four kinds of forgiveness and how you can master each one:

1. Beginning forgiveness of yourself: Be compassionate toward yourself for doing the best you could with the resources you had at the time, make amends, and then release the situation.

2. Beginning forgiveness of another: Identify with that person's motivation so you can understand why she did what she did, show compassion, and then release it.

3. Advanced forgiveness of yourself: Understand why you did what you did, make amends as best as you can, then find it in your heart to absolve yourself.

4. Advanced forgiveness of another: Allow yourself to fully feel the hurt or anger so that you can release it, then view the situation as a necessary part of your path of spiritual evolution.

ETHICS

"There are no mistakes, no coincidences. All events are blessings given to us to learn from."

Elisabeth Kübler-Ross

So you made what you perceived to be a mistake, you eventually forgave yourself, made amends, and released the situation from your mind. You will still be left with one lingering lesson: the importance of ethics. Morality is conforming to the established standards of right and wrong that have been set by the society in which you live. But ethical codes are not universal. There is no one set of guidelines that works for everyone around the world, since what we may consider morally wrong in one culture might be acceptable in another. For some, ethics are defined by religious laws. For others, moral codes arise from lessons learned in school or from parents. Most people in our culture were raised with the Golden Rule, "Do unto others as you would have them do unto you."

At its most basic, ethics involves choosing right or good behavior in your relationships with others. You are constantly strengthening your ability to choose between right or wrong. While we have basic ethics instilled in us and know what is right and what is wrong in our hearts, life throws many situations at us where what is right is not always apparent. Life is complicated and full of gray areas. Each and every situation you find yourself in forces you to choose between the two. For example, when you were in school you may have questioned whether it was right or wrong to let your friend cheat off you on a test. Your friend may have been unprepared for the test because she was having troubles at home. You knew it was wrong to let her cheat but if you didn't, she would have failed the test and had even more problems to deal with.

When your external actions reflect your internal code, you are in alignment with your morality. This is how an individual gains integrity. Integrity is important because without it you are living with a sense of division within yourself; you feel incomplete and conflicted.

You will know when you are not acting in alignment with your moral code, because your conscience will remind you of the difference between what is ethically right and how you actually behaved. You will most likely experience feelings of guilt or remorse that will serve as a clue to you that the lesson of ethics needs to be learned. Whether or not you are discovered and punished for wrong behavior does not matter. You will instinctually know that you behaved wrongly. You may have only yourself to answer to, but isn't your conscience a powerful teacher, if you listen to it?

Antonio dearly loved his wife Cynthia. He was a

devoted husband, and their life was truly blessed with harmony and compatibility.

One weekend, while they were away at a wedding for some close friends, something happened that threatened their idyllic life. Antonio found himself lusting after Cynthia's friend Vivian, and, unable to contain his attraction, leaned over and kissed Vivian while the two were alone in the elevator in the hotel. Vivian returned his kiss, and they stood there, pressed up against the wall with their arms around each other for several moments. Then, suddenly, as if cold water were thrown on him, Antonio abruptly came to his senses, pulled away, and exclaimed, "What am I doing? I'm sorry. I don't know what came over me. I have always been attracted to you, but this isn't right. I'm very sorry." Without hesitation, they agreed to dismiss the encounter as if it never happened. They exited the elevator and went back to their respective rooms.

Antonio was devastated. How could he have done such a thing, he wondered to himself. He knew he loved Cynthia more than anything in the world, and he was horrified by his actions. Riddled with shame and self-disgust, Antonio spent the rest of the weekend stewing.

Sunday night, in the airport, as they waited for their plane home, Antonio was still tormented by guilt. The internal schism he had created between his ethics and his actions plagued his conscience, and he could not look his beloved wife in the eye. He finally decided to confess to her, knowing that although the truth could destroy his marriage and radically alter his entire life, he needed to be honest with Cynthia. After telling her what had happened, he apologized profusely for his behavior and begged for her forgiveness.

Cynthia was shocked, hurt, and angry. After taking some time to sort out her feelings, however, she was able to find the forgiveness in her heart to release the event and absolve Antonio of his transgression. They were both relieved that their relationship had a solid enough foundation to withstand this test.

Although Cynthia's forgiveness made Antonio's heart ache a little less, he still needed to live with the internal repercussions of his lack of integrity. He had violated his own ethics, and even though he made amends for the wrong he had caused, he would eventually need to forgive himself so that the gap between his ethics and his actions could close and he could be free from his shame and guilt. Over time, Antonio did, in fact, release the guilt, but the memory of how horrible he felt that night in the airport stayed to remind him to not stray again from his own ethics.

HUMOR

"It is of immense importance to learn to laugh at ourselves."

Katherine Mansfield

The lesson of humor means learning to invite levity and amusement into situations that might otherwise be disastrous. If you are going to view the hardships that happen to you or the slip-ups you make as lessons rather than mistakes, a sense of humor will prove helpful. When you learn to laugh at your mishaps you are able to instantaneously transform perceived bad situations into opportunities to learn something about the absurdity of human behavior, most especially your own!

Humor and laughter are also tremendously important in relationships. Sharing a good laugh with someone does wonders. A friend of mine told me that once when she and her husband were having a disagreement he made a face that struck her as so comical, she burst out laughing. They both realized how silly they were being and they were able to share a laugh and resolve their conflict with a new perspective. As Victor Borge said, "Laughter is the closest distance between two people."

The health benefits, both mental and physical, of humor are well documented. A good laugh can diffuse tension, relieve stress, and release endorphins into your system, which act as a natural mood elevator. In Norman Cousins's book, *Anatomy of an Illness*, Cousins describes the regimen he followed to overcome a serious, debilitating disease he was suffering from. It included large doses of laughter and humor. Published in 1976, his book has been widely read and accepted by the medical community.

Laughter causes misery to vanish. It teaches you to lighten up and take yourself less seriously, even in the most serious of situations. It can also help you gain some much needed perspective. A young woman named Alisa spent close to a year planning her wedding. She and her fiancé invited over three hundred guests to what was to be a lavish, formal affair in a beautiful banquet hall. She wanted it to be perfect, so she paid close attention to every last detail, right down to the cocktail napkins.

The big day came and everything went brilliantly until the very expensive wedding cake was rolled out. A wheel of the table got caught on a wire, and the cake went flying through the air, finally landing in a big chocolate-and-icing splattered mess on the dance floor. All the guests held their breath as they looked at Alisa, expecting her to burst into tears. Much to everyone's surprise, she looked down at the cake, started to laugh, and joked, "Hey, I ordered a *vanilla* cake!"

So give yourself permission to laugh. You'll be amazed at how quickly a crisis can turn into a comedy when you invite in humor.

A LESSON
IS REPEATED
UNTIL LEARNED

*Lessons will be repeated to you in various forms until
you have learned them. When you have learned them,
you can then go on to the next lesson.*

Have you ever noticed that lessons tend to repeat themselves? Does it seem as if you married or dated the same person several times in different bodies with different names? Have you run into the same type of boss over and over again? Do you find yourself having the same problem with many different coworkers?

Several years ago, Bill Murray starred in a movie called *Groundhog Day*, in which he woke up in the same day over and over until he learned all the lessons he needed to in that one day. The same events kept repeating themselves until he finally "got" what it was he was supposed to do in each one. Does this strike a funny but familiar chord with you?

Lessons will be repeated until learned. When I taught high school, I always told my students, "If you don't deal well with authority figures at home, then you will have an opportunity to deal with them out in the world. You will continually draw into your life people who need to enforce authority, and you will struggle with them until you learn the lesson of obedience." Teenagers often perceive their parents as overly strict. At the age of fourteen, one of my former students went away to boarding school. Much to her surprise, she found teachers and staff with the same rules that her mother had laid down at home and that I had at school. She finally understood.

In couples' counseling it is often noted that people who divorce and remarry nearly always marry the same type of person they just left. Similarly, a friend of mine named Cassidy who was a compulsive perfectionist had a knack for attracting inappropriate men. It was no coincidence that Cassidy, to whom mismatched socks were a horror and a torn shirt a federal offense, repeatedly drew men into her life who dressed like slobs. She was a stickler for manners, yet her most recent boyfriend held his spoon like Fred Flintstone wields a drumstick. Only recently did Cassidy begin to acknowledge that perhaps these men were appearing in her life as teachers and opportunities to work out her perfectionist issue.

You will continually attract the same lesson into

your life. You will also draw to you teachers to teach you that lesson until you get it right. The only way you can free yourself of difficult patterns and issues you tend to repeat is by shifting your perspective so that you can recognize the patterns and learn the lessons that they offer. You may try to avoid the situations, but they will eventually catch up with you.

To face these challenges means you need to accept the fact that something within you keeps drawing you to the same kind of person or issue, painful though that situation or relationship may be. In the words of Carl Jung, "There is no coming to consciousness without pain." And come to consciousness you must if you are ever to stop repeating the same lessons and be able to move on to new ones.

The challenge of Rule Four is to identify and release the patterns that you are repeating. As any good facilitator or therapist will tell you, this is no easy task, since it means you have to change, and change is not always easy. Staying just as you are may not help you advance spiritually, but it certainly is comfortable in its familiarity. You grooved your patterns a long time ago as a way of protecting yourself. Moving into unfamiliar new behavior can be uncomfortable not to mention at times frightening.

Rising to the challenge of identifying and releasing your patterns forces you to admit that the way you have been doing things isn't working. The good news is that by identifying and releasing the pattern, you actually learn how to change.

In my seminars, I teach that there are **six** basic steps to executing any change in your life. They are:

1. awareness—becoming conscious of the pattern or issue

2. acknowledgment—admitting that you need to release the pattern

3. choice—actively selecting to release the pattern

4. strategy—creating a realistic plan

5. commitment—taking action, aided by external accountability

6. celebration—rewarding yourself for succeeding

No lasting change can be made, nor any pattern released permanently, without going through each one of these steps. In order to facilitate your process of change, you will need to learn the lessons of awareness, willingness, causality, and patience. Once you master these, you will most likely find the challenge of identifying and releasing your patterns far less intimidating.

AWARENESS

"Only that day dawns to which we are awake."

Henry David Thoreau

Awareness is the process of becoming fully conscious. Awareness can trickle into the corners of your mind slowly, as you clean out the cobwebs, or it can dawn suddenly the moment you become cognizant of your patterns and begin to see yourself objectively. However it is attained, it is like a light-bulb being switched on that illuminates the dark pockets of your unconscious mind. It is the first step to facilitating any change you wish to make in yourself.

Cultivating awareness is a lifelong process. Every moment presents you with the opportunity to remain awake or to slip into unconscious behavior. We can walk through life on "automatic pilot" or we can pay attention and behave in a conscious manner. The key to learning awareness lies in tracing the root of your behaviors so you can identify the beliefs that cause you to repeat the same patterns. Once you identify the patterns, you can then work on releasing them through willingness.

The opportunity to learn the lesson of awareness is presented each time you feel a sense of discontent in your life. With every desire for a shift in your path, or vision of something different, comes the chance to look within and ask yourself, "What is the truth of what I want? What change do I want to make?" The answer that arises to those questions will provide you with the awareness you need to move forward in your process of change.

There are countless ways to awaken. Paying attention to your feelings is the easiest way to get in touch with your inner machinations. Feelings are the lights on the dashboard of life; when one is illuminated, you can be sure it is a signal of some internal issue that needs to be addressed.

Simply noticing your behavior can bring you to awareness. When you observe your actions as an objective spectator, you remove the filter of self-judgment and allow yourself to see the patterns that you are repeating. As you watch yourself in a variety of situations and notice similar actions and reactions, you bring to light the common thread attached to the necessary lesson.

Tools like meditation, journal writing, personal coaching, and therapy help many learn awareness. For others, simply posting meaningful reminders on the bathroom mirror works. For me, surrounding myself with others who are on their path and live in a conscious way is the best way to stay awake.

Since lessons are repeated until learned, and since you cannot learn lessons until you become aware of them, it makes sense that you will need to cultivate awareness if you are to ever progress from where you are right now on your path. Ask yourself what patterns you are repeating; you might be surprised to see how evident they were all along.

WILLINGNESS

"Life doesn't require that we be the best—only that we try our best."

H. Jackson Brown Jr.

The real secret to being able to change is the willingness to do so. If you are to make any progress at all in excavating yourself from the cycles that entrap you, you must first identify the patterns that keep you stuck. Then you can begin to release the old behaviors.

If you truly *want* to change, you will *choose* to do it, and make a commitment to the process of it. However, if you rely on the thought that you *should* change, you will make the *decision* to do so and then you will feel the pinch of sacrifice. Following the current trends, the advice of friends, or the wishes of family members result in decisions; following your inner compass results in choice.

Perhaps the change you wish to make is to stop smoking. If you truly *want* to stop, then you *choose* to do so, and you make a *commitment* to quitting. However, if you just have the nagging feeling that you *should* quit, you might then *decide* to do so, and thus end up feeling like you are making a *sacrifice* by quitting.

Or perhaps you think you need to begin an exercise regime. If you truly *want* to do this because you want to become healthier or more fit, then you will viscerally make the *choice* to do so, and you will have a much easier time making a *commitment* to your new routine. However, if you think you *should* exercise to look or feel better, you will most likely *decide* to do so somewhat half-heartedly and thus feel like you are making a *sacrifice* each time you try to exercise.

Remember:
WANT leads to CHOICE, which leads to
    COMMITMENT.
SHOULD leads to DECISION, which leads to
    SACRIFICE.

Whenever I think of the lesson of willingness, I think of a woman named Karen who came to one of my time management workshops. Karen was an incredibly busy person who ran around all the time trying to catch up on all the things she had to do. Between her errands, phone calls, hectic job, and social obligations, Karen was always on the run and never on time for anything.

Karen's family began to get angry that she rarely had time for them, and that when she did make time, she would show up nearly an hour late. Her boss admonished her repeatedly for arriving late to work. Her friends felt ignored and annoyed that she could not even send their birthday cards on time. The pressure on Karen to change her ways was enormous, so she decided to work on managing her time better.

Karen did improve her habits—for about a week. She tried to organize her time better so that everyone in her life would be happy, but she overlooked one essential fact: she really did not *want* to change. She was not willing to give up the adrenaline rush she got from running around all the time. She enjoyed feeling needed in many different places at once. Giving that up felt like a sacrifice to her. Karen's efforts to change fell short, and she ultimately reverted to her old patterns.

By the time Karen came to the workshop, several months after her aborted attempt to change, she was physically exhausted and emotionally drained. She herself could no longer tolerate living the way she had been living. Karen admitted she needed to change, not for anyone else's sake, but for her own sanity. Karen was willing to change, and thus *chose* to do so. She no longer wanted to miss the first hour of every family dinner or have to sneak in the back door of her office building in the morning. It was her willingness that allowed her to commit to a more manageable schedule and eventually get her life under control.

So the next time you are struggling to make a change in your life, ask yourself, "How willing am I, really, to make this change?" If you are not succeeding, there's a good chance that you may be relying on your belief that you *should* change, rather than on your intrinsic desire to do so.

CAUSALITY

"To every action there is always opposed an equal reaction."

Sir Isaac Newton

Causality is the acknowledgment that you are the source of your manifestations. In other words, everything that you attract into your life is coming to you because of something you are projecting out into the world, and you are therefore responsible for drawing to you all of your circumstances. It's difficult to give up the idea that circumstances just happen *to* you, as opposed to *because* of you or your behavior. By remaining an innocent victim of fate, you do not have to acknowledge that you are in any way responsible for what befalls you, and you can continue to hide deep within the vortex of your patterns.

Think back to my friend the perfectionist who consistently attracted sloppy men into her life. As she and I discussed her pattern, she began to consider the possibility that she was projecting something out into the world that was attracting these men. Perhaps it was that she was so well put together and groomed that they gravitated toward her, so that she could reinforce their identity as slobs by comparison. Or perhaps it was simply an issue of chemistry. Regardless of what energy it was that drew these men into her life, she ultimately needed to own up to the fact that she was the cause of her circumstances.

Or let's look at Andrew, a chef who had gotten fired from four different restaurants for inappropriate behavior. In each case, he claimed that the management of the restaurant was to blame. He either said he had been victimized by the management, "set up" by his boss, or not told exactly what it was he was supposed to do. What Andrew needed to look at, however, was the behavior that he was repeating over and over that was causing the pattern to perpetuate. That is not to say that each firing was entirely his fault; it just seems highly unlikely that four different restaurants could have the same issue with him without there being some truth to it. Andrew needed to learn that he played a role in creating his circumstances. Then and only then could he begin to see his pattern and work to release it.

PATIENCE

"Be patient. You'll know when it's time for you to wake up and move ahead."

Ram Dass

Patience is the display of tolerance while awaiting an outcome. You are presented with the lesson of patience the moment you try to create a change within yourself. You expect immediate results and are often disappointed when your first few attempts to follow through fall short. When people who try to lose weight cheat on their diets, they get very frustrated with themselves for not being able to stay with their new eating regime and berate themselves for not changing their patterns.

As you already know, change is rarely easy, and you need to exercise gentleness and patience with yourself as you work your way through this process. Growth can be a slow, painstaking process and patience will provide you with the stamina you need to become the person you want to be.

If you absolutely hate getting stuck in traffic, chances are you need a little work in the area of patience. And, chances are, you will probably get stuck in more traffic jams than someone who has no issue with patience—and not simply because the universe has a sense of humor. You will just notice the traffic more than someone who has no issues with it.

Remember, a lesson will be repeated until learned. It just takes a little patience.

Rule Five

LEARNING DOES NOT END

There is no part of life that does not contain lessons.
If you are alive, there are lessons to
be learned.

Does it ever seem like just when you have mastered one lesson, another challenge presents itself almost immediately? Just when you get what it means to possess self-esteem, you are faced with a lesson in humility. As soon as you get what it means to be a good parent, your children leave home and you need to learn the lesson of letting go. You figure out one day the importance of having time to yourself, and the next day you are called to support someone else. Striving to get all the details of life under control is impossible, because life will present new lessons daily.

You never actually finish all your lessons, for as

long as you are alive, there are lessons to learn. Regardless of your age, or station in life, or success level, you will never be exempt from the lessons you need to learn in order to continue growing. Your journey on Earth is constantly unfolding, and while your wisdom grows and your capacity to deal with challenges expands, new lessons will present themselves. In fact, as the depth of your wisdom increases, your capacities expand proportionately, allowing you to take on and solve with greater ease more advanced challenges.

It may come as a relief to finally understand that you never actually master life, and that striving to do so will only lead to frustration. The best you can do is strive to master the process by which you experience it. Life is a year-round school from which you never actually graduate, so it is the learning process itself that brings true value to existence.

The challenge of Rule Five is to embrace your role as a perpetual student of life. This means giving in to the idea that you actually don't know everything that you need to, and you never will. It also means that you need to convince your ego that being a student does not make you inferior. In fact, being a student opens up worlds of possibilities that are invisible to those who are unwilling to accept this role.

In order to rise to the challenge of embracing your role as perpetual student, you need to learn the lessons of surrender, commitment, humility, and flexibility. Without these important lessons, you will never be able to open your mind, heart, and spirit wide enough to allow yourself to take in all that life has to teach you.

SURRENDER

"Surrender doesn't obstruct our power; it enhances it."

Marianne Williamson

Surrender is the transcendence of ego and the release of control. When you surrender to your lessons that arise, you allow yourself to flow with the rhythm of life, rather than struggling against it. The peaks and valleys that mark your personal path become easier to traverse when you surrender to them.

The key to coming to peace with your role as a perpetual student lies in surrendering to what *is*, rather than trying to create what you envision *should be*. If resistance has been a theme throughout your life, then surrender will appear in your curriculum. If you are one of those people who always have to do things his way or who possess a strong, willful ego, then surrender will seem like defeat to you. But surrender only signifies defeat in war. In life it signifies transcendence.

This is not to say that you should remain passive

and just let life happen to you. Rather, you need to learn to surrender to those circumstances over which you never really had any control anyway. Ironically, as I was working on this very chapter, I had one of those tragic computer glitches, in which I lost twelve pages of material. The moment the screen went blank, I knew I was being tested. I had a choice: I could either get very upset over the lost material, or just surrender to the fact that it was gone and start over. Either way—surrender or no surrender—*the reality remained the same.* The material was gone whether I surrendered to that fact or became upset about it. Would I have preferred to have not lost all those hours of work? Of course. But there was absolutely nothing I could do about it, so I chose to bypass the drama, went for a walk to clear my head, and then came back to rewrite the lost pages.

If you surrender to the fact that the universe will always present you with lessons, over and over again, you can stop trying to second-guess the divine plan. You will be amazed how much easier life gets when you stop resisting and controlling it, and ride the waves toward the fulfillment of your destiny.

COMMITMENT

"Our greatest weakness lies in giving up. The most certain way to succeed is always to try just one more time."

Thomas Edison

Commitment means devoting yourself to something or someone and staying with it—no matter what. If you look at anyone who is a good student, you will see a shining example of commitment. He or she is fully devoted to his or her course of study and commits to it all the time and energy that is needed to excel. As you come to embrace your role as a matriculating student, you need to make a commitment to yourself and the universe to learning and mastering all your lessons.

If you have this lesson in your life path, it will show up as an inability to make choices or to stick to choices already made. It might start with the difficulty in choosing ice cream flavors, grow into a dilemma about how to spend your free time, then get compounded by where to live. If you still haven't learned the lesson by adulthood, it could manifest in ambivalence about marrying the person you've been dating for eight years. If you spend twenty minutes agonizing over whether to order a tuna sandwich on rye or whole wheat, then commitment is definitely a lesson you need to learn.

Molly, a widow living in Florida, had been alone

for six years when she decided she wanted to find a new partner. So, at the age of seventy-five, she started dating again for the first time in fifty years. But instead of taking the attitude that she didn't need or want to learn anything new at her age, Molly enthusiastically committed to learning a whole new set of lessons that are essential to anyone who is dating. When a man who she liked never called after their first date, she needed to relearn the lesson of self-esteem. When she met a gentleman who acted rudely toward her, she needed to remember the lesson of compassion. When she consistently attracted men who did not want to be in committed relationships, she needed to reexamine the lesson of causality. It was her commitment to continue learning that kept her going and eventually led her to Morty, a seventy-eight-year-old retired insurance salesman who shared her love of golf and Chinese food. I am happy to say that Molly and Morty are currently planning their wedding.

HUMILITY

"And when you have reached the mountain top, then you shall begin to climb."

Kahlil Gibran

A person with humility has a confident yet modest sense of his or her own merits, but also an understanding of his or her limitations. The moment you think you have seen everything or know it all ("Been there, done that . . ."), the universe senses arrogance and gives you a great big dose of humility. You must give up on the idea that you can ever become so enlightened that you have nothing left to learn; Zen masters know that even for them learning never ends.

Humility is the lesson that stings, for along with it usually comes some kind of loss or downfall. The universe likes to keep things in balance, so when an inflated ego ignores civility and patience, it introduces humility as a way to bring the ego back down to Earth. Though the sting feels like a wound at the time, it really is just a poke from the higher power to keep you balanced.

Some people experience so much success in life that they take it for granted, expecting things to go their way automatically. When this results in an inflated ego that ignores patience and civility, arrogance is bred, and humility becomes a curriculum requirement. That is what happened to Will.

Extremely handsome, tan, and athletic, with penetrating eyes, Will looked and dressed like a fashion model. Things came easily to him, and he mastered everything he tried. With his charm, intelligence, and talents, his business was lively and success was a way of life.

So when Will was served a lawsuit one day, he

assumed that the case would work out as easily as everything else in his life and he didn't worry about it. But it didn't, and the suit eventually led to the breakup of his company. He tried for months afterward to get a job, but no one would hire him. His finances became strained, payments fell behind, and finally bankruptcy was his only option. Will couldn't understand why his "magic" was no longer intact, and after seven years of assorted jobs that yielded no magic, he finally faced up to the lesson of humility.

When he came to see me, Will couldn't understand how so much misfortune could come to a "perfect person" like him. He had to learn that his talents were wonderful but were negated alongside an attitude of arrogance. He looked condescendingly upon people who didn't have his gifts—speaking to them in a patronizing manner, treating them with impatience and annoyance, judging them as worthless or stupid—so his curriculum led him to the lesson of humility. Over time, Will came to understand why life had given him so many intense lessons in humility. The lessons were difficult for him at first but with understanding, Will made sense of his situation and committed to learning his lessons, and he turned his circumstances around.

Have pride in who you are and what you have accomplished. However, if you find yourself harboring secret thoughts of arrogance or conceit, remind yourself of the lesson of humility before the universe does it for you. It will sting much less that way.

FLEXIBILITY

"To improve is to change; to be perfect is to change often."

Winston Churchill

Flexibility is defined as being adaptable to change. In the course of your lifetime, you will be tempted to try to hold on to *what is*, when in fact, *what is* is only a temporary phase that evolves almost immediately into *what was*. It is essential that you learn to bend and flex around every new circumstance, as rigidity robs you of the opportunity to see the freedom of new possibilities.

In order to truly embrace your role as a student of life, you need to cultivate the ability to move easily from "knowingness" to "not-knowingness," which in turn moves you from master to student again and again. In other words, you learn the lesson of flexibility once you are able to flow with what is coming next rather than clinging to the way things are presently.

Paradigms change over time, and so must you. Your company may restructure, and you will have to survive. Your spouse may choose to leave the marriage, and you will have to cope. Technology will con-

tinue to advance and change, and you must constantly
learn and adapt or risk becoming a dinosaur. Flexibility allows you to be ready for whatever curve lies
ahead in life instead of getting blindsided by it.

From 1900 to 1967, the Swiss were the leading
watchmakers in the world. In 1967, when the digital technology was patented by the Swiss, they
rejected it in favor of the traditional ball bearings,
gears, and mainsprings they had been using to make
watches for decades. Unfortunately, however, the
world was ready for this advance, and Seiko, a Japa-
nese company, picked up the digital patent and
became the leading watch manufacturer in the world
almost overnight. Fifty thousand of the 67,000
Swiss watchmakers went out of business because
they refused to embrace this new technology. It was
not until years later that the Swiss caught up and
regained their position in the marketplace with the
creation of Swatch watches.

Learn to be flexible; it makes the curves in your
life path much easier to maneuver.

"THERE" IS
NO BETTER
THAN "HERE"

*When your "there" has become a "here," you will
simply obtain a "there" that will look better to you
than your present "here."*

Many people believe that they will be happy once they arrive at some specific goal they set for themselves. For some the goal may be amassing a million dollars, for others losing those annoying ten-plus pounds, and for still others it is finding a soulmate. It could be getting a better job, driving a nicer car, or pursuing a dream career. Whatever your "there" is, you may be convinced that once you arrive you will finally find the peace you have always dreamed of. You will finally become fulfilled, happy, generous, loving, and content.

However, more often than not, once you arrive "there" you will still feel dissatisfied, and move your "there" vision to yet another point in the future. By always chasing after another "there," you are never really appreciating what you already have right "here." Think of past situations in which you said, "I will be happy when..." and then ask yourself, "Was I really any happier when I actually arrived there?" Perhaps for a brief moment, but the same longing arises, and you must embark on yet another new quest.

By continuously engaging a cycle of longing, you never actually allow yourself to *be* in the present. You end up living your life at some point just off in the future. You only have one moment—the one right here, right now. If you skip over "here" in your rush to get "there," you deny yourself the full range of feelings and sensations that can only be experienced in the present moment.

The challenge of Rule Six is to live in the present. Spiritual teachers from the beginning of time have struggled with the question of how we can live in the present moment—a challenge that has become particularly difficult in the modern world in which we are constantly lured by visions of greater glory, beauty, fame, or fortune and bombarded by unattainable images of how we should strive to be.

It is important to recognize that being human means coming to terms with the age-old drive to look beyond the place where you now stand. On one hand, your life is enhanced by your dreams and aspirations. These are what drive you forward and keep your passions alive, not to mention enable society to evolve.

On the other hand, these drives can pull you farther and farther from your enjoyment of your life right now. In formal education and your job, as well as in your private life, goal setting is a necessary skill. There is nothing wrong with wanting to improve your circumstances. Your challenge is to focus on the present, and on what we have right now, while simultaneously holding the intention of your future goals.

The secret is to dance on the fine line between living in the here and now while holding in your heart your fondest dreams and aspirations for the future. By learning the lessons of gratitude, unattachment, abundance, and peace, you can bring yourself closer to fulfilling the challenge of living in the present.

GRATITUDE

"When you stop comparing what is right here and now with what you wish were, you can begin to enjoy what is."

Cheri Huber

To be grateful means you are thankful for and appreciative of what you have and where you are on your path right now. Gratitude fills your heart with the joyful feeling of being blessed with many gifts and allows you to fully appreciate everything that arises on your path. As you strive to keep your focus on the present moment, you can experience the full wonder of "here."

My friend Martin always used to complain about the city of Los Angeles, where he lived for three years while getting his doctorate. He complained incessantly about the smog, the traffic, and the expensive lifestyle. Martin was convinced life would be far rosier when he would be able to move to another city.

Within a few weeks of finishing his program and earning his degree, Martin packed his belongings and moved to Boulder. Within months of his arrival there, he began to complain about the cold weather, the slow pace, and how much difficulty he was having finding a house that was up to his standards. Suddenly, he regretted that he never appreciated the sunny weather and the exciting lifestyle of Los Angeles. In my last conversation with Martin, I gently pointed out that perhaps this was an opportunity for him to learn the lesson of gratitude by appreciating the splendor of his new city, rather than focusing on another "there."

Gratitude is a lesson that needs to be reinforced often. It is too easy to overlook the gifts you have when you focus on those that you hope to obtain, and you diminish the value of where you currently are on your path if you do not pause often to appreciate it.

There are many ways to cultivate gratitude. Here are just a few suggestions you may wish to try:

- Imagine what your life would be like if you lost all that you had. Like George Bailey in the movie *It's a Wonderful Life,* this will most surely remind you of how much you do appreciate it.

- Make a list each day of all that you are grateful for, so that you can stay conscious daily of your blessings. Do this especially when you are feeling as though you have nothing to feel grateful for. Or spend a few minutes before you go to sleep giving thanks for all that you have.

- Spend time offering assistance to those who are less fortunate than you, so that you may gain perspective.

- Look for the gift in each challenging incident.

However you choose to learn gratitude is irrelevent. What really matters is that you create a space in your consciousness for appreciation for all that you have right now, so that you may live more joyously in your present moment.

UNATTACHMENT

"Perhaps the hardest lesson to learn is not to be attached to the results of your actions."

Joan Borysenko

Unattachment is the release of need or expectation associated with a specific outcome. For most people, this is one of the most difficult lessons to learn. We become attached to the way we envision something working out, and struggle to make circumstances bend to our desires. Life, however, often has its own agenda, and we are destined to suffer unless we give up our attachment to things working out exactly as we would like. We learn unattachment when we are able to release our belief that "there" is any better than "here."

Unattachment is one of the cornerstones of Buddhism. For centuries Buddhists have taught that one of the major causes of unhappiness is desire— desire for a person, for material things, for money or status. These desires create our attachments. We become attached to a person, attached to money, our new car, or our status as a senior vice president. Ultimately these attachments are fleeting, we spend a lot of our time and energy in pursuit of them, and they prevent us from paying attention to the really important things in life. Feeling desire assumes a sense of dissatisfaction and brings about suffering.

The way to happiness is to eliminate desire and the way to eliminate desire is to eliminate attachments.

Being unattached does not mean being disinterested or removed; rather, it means remaining neutral in your judgments of circumstances and in your desire for a specific outcome. In other words, if your goal is to amass a million dollars, it is natural and right for you to pursue that goal. The key to serenity, however, lies in your ability to hold lightly to the image of yourself reaching that goal. In doing so you will feel peaceful in your situation regardless of the outcome. Unattachment means you are not bound by your expectations of how things should turn out, and that you are willing to let go.

In order to learn how to dissolve attachments, you will need to take the following steps:

1. Notice what you want and acknowledge the outcome you are attached to.

2. Imagine the ideal outcome of your situation, and then imagine the worst-case scenario. Doing this brings any hidden fears to light and makes it acceptable for the outcome to go either way.

3. Make a clear statement to the universe by writing out your desire clearly or saying it out loud.

4. In your mind, create the image of you holding the intention lightly in the palm of

your hand, with your fingers held loosely
open.

5. Mentally release the desire out into the universe, trusting that whatever outcome you
receive will be the right one. You can use the
visualization of placing your wish in a
helium balloon and allowing the balloon to
drift up and away. Actually see yourself letting go of the attachment.

If your desire is for financial prosperity, your
first step would be to notice your desire and
acknowledge any attachments you have to achieving
such prosperity. Perhaps you envision in your
mind's eye an easier life, filled with abundant luxu-
ries and many hours of free time, and you believe
that financial prosperity will afford you that life.
Become very clear in your mind about the outcome
you believe you will experience if you realize your
desire.

Run your mind through the worst-case scenario. What would happen if you did not achieve
financial prosperity? Take this to the furthest
extreme you can imagine, even it sounds far-
fetched and irrational. Doing this will bring your
deepest fears and beliefs to light and give them
less of a hold over you.

Next, put your intention of achieving financial
prosperity out into the universe, through mental

images, thoughts, words—perhaps even in writing. Be specific and clear about what you want.

Third, conjure up the picture in your mind of you holding financial prosperity lightly in the palm of your hand, with your fingers outstretched.

Then release your desire out into the universe, mentally envisioning it encased in a helium balloon, floating away. Remain anchored in the knowledge that whatever outcome you receive will ultimately be for the best.

If your desire is to get married, you would take these steps:

1. Notice the desire to find a partner and get married.

2. Acknowledge the attachments you have to getting married. Perhaps you believe you will feel safe, or secure, or blissful. Perhaps you believe your life will truly begin, or that you will find the love of which you have always dreamed.

3. Now imagine the worst-case scenario, in which your desire is not realized. What would happen if you never met your soulmate and never got married? Take this as far as your imagination allows, even if it takes you to images of yourself alone forever. Bring any and all horrible fears to light; this will give them less weight.

4. State, imagine, or write your desire to meet your soulmate and get married. Put it out into the universe in a clear, direct way.

5. Hold the intention and image of yourself getting married in your mind. Picture yourself balancing that image in the palm of your open hand.

6. Visualize releasing the image and all of your attachments to it. Know that the universe will provide you with whatever you need for growth in terms of realizing this desire.

Pay attention to the motivations behind your attachments. You may be attached to getting married or rich because you think it will bring about security. The fact is being rich or married in no way guarantees a secure life free of worries. It may actually make you *less* secure. A sense of security comes from within, not from attachment to any person, thing, or idea.

It is important to recognize that your desire or intention may also show up in a form different from that which you might have expected. For example, if your desire is prosperity, it may not come in the form of a winning lottery ticket, but more indirectly, like in the form of a lucrative job offer. If your desire is to find a soulmate, you might be sent a wonderful new friend to fill your need to connect with someone in lieu of a lover. Keep your eyes wide open for gifts from the universe, as they sometimes come in unexpected packages.

ABUNDANCE

"The richest person is the one who is contented with what he has."

Robert C. Savage

One of the most common human fears is scarcity. Many people are afraid of not having enough of whatever it is they need or want, and so they are always striving to get to some point in the future when they finally have enough. They fool themselves into believing that one day they will have everything "all set"—they will have all the money they need, all the possessions they desire, all the love they crave, all the success they strive for. But is anything ever really enough? Did anyone ever really arrive "there"?

Abundance means that all things are possible and that there is more than enough of everything for everyone, right here and now. As you shift your focus from some point in the future to the present, you are able to fully see the riches and gifts you already have, and thus learn the lesson of abundance.

Alan and Linda always dreamed of living "the good life." Both from poor working-class families, they married young and set out to fulfill their mutual goal of becoming wealthy. They both worked very hard for years, amassing a small fortune, so they could move from their two-bedroom condominium to a palatial seven-bedroom home in the most upscale neighborhood in their community. They focused their energies on accumulating all the things they believed signified abundance: membership in the local exclusive country club, luxury cars, designer clothing, and high-class society friends. No matter how much they accumulated, however, it never seemed to be enough. They were unable to erase the deep fear of scarcity both had acquired in childhood. They needed to learn the lesson of abundance.

Then the stock market crashed in 1987, and Alan and Linda lost a considerable amount of money. A bizarre but costly lawsuit depleted another huge portion of their savings. One thing led to another, and they found themselves in a financial tailspin. Assets needed to be sold to pay bills, and eventually they lost the country club membership, the cars, and the house.

It took several years and much hard work for Alan and Linda to land on their feet, and though they now live a life far from extravagant, they have taken stock of their lives and feel quite blessed. Only now, as they assess what they have left—a solid, loving marriage, their health, a dependable income, and good friends—do they realize that true abundance comes not from amassing, but rather from appreciating.

Scarcity consciousness arises as a result of what I call the "hole-in-the-soul syndrome." This is when we attempt to fill the gaps in our inner lives with things from the outside world. But like puzzle pieces, you can't fit something in where it does not naturally belong. No amount of external objects, affection, love, or attention can ever fill an inner void. The void can only be filled by looking within. You already have and are enough; revel in your own interior abundance and you will never need to look elsewhere.

PEACE

"There is nothing to do but be."
    Stephen Levine

Living in the present brings the one thing most people spend their lives striving to achieve: peace. Relaxing into the present moment puts you in the mental and physical state of calm, quiet, and tranquillity and finally gets us off the here-but-gotta-get-there treadmill. If you are in the moment doing whatever you are doing, then there is no time to examine the gap between your expectation and the reality of how things are, or between where you are and where you think you should be. You are too busy being *in* the moment to *analyze* it and find fault with it.

One of my favorite movies is *Being There,* in which Peter Sellers plays the lovable idiot savant Chauncey Gardner. Simple-minded Chauncey lives his life only in the present moment, with absolutely no awareness of anything other than what he sees before him. When an odd twist of circumstances transports him from his beloved garden, which he spent most of his life tending, into a position advising presidents and powerful business moguls, Chauncey merely offers the wisdom he gleaned from tending the flowers and soil. Of course, the rest of the world interprets his simple statements as wise analogies, and he is hailed as one of the greatest minds of our time.

Chauncey is peaceful in his simplicity. Life is simple and easy for this man, to whom past and future references have no meaning. He is focused completely on the present moment.

Many of us race through our lives, always on our way somewhere. If you ask ten drivers on their morning commute what they are doing, nine of them will most likely respond, "going to work." The tenth one—the one who responds, "driving my car"—is the one who has learned the lesson of present-moment peace. Chances are he does not arrive at work any later than the other nine who spent their commute focused on where they were headed as opposed to where they were. He probably even enjoyed the ride.

Of course, I am not suggesting that you float through your life, completely detached from the past and blind to the future. Only that you pause from time to time to be fully rooted in the moment and feel the peace that results.

OTHERS ARE
ONLY MIRRORS
OF YOU

*You cannot love or hate something about another
person unless it reflects something you love or hate
about yourself.*

The first time you meet someone, in the first
moment you form an impression in your mind
of that person. You decide within the first four minutes what you like and don't like. These decisions are
based on details that your senses tell you, such as the
person's eye color or cologne scent, or on past experiences stored in your memory bank that you associ-
ate with this person.

Your reactions to other people, however, are
really just barometers for how you perceive yourself.
Your reactions to others say more about you than
they do about others. You cannot really love or hate
something about another person unless it reflects

something you love or hate about yourself. We are usually drawn to those who are most like us and tend to dislike those who display those aspects of ourselves that we dislike. We view others through the grid of our past experiences, feelings, and thoughts. Usually we convince ourselves that our perceptions of them are objective and disconnected to any of our own issues.

Consider, however, approaching your life as if other people were mirroring back to you important information. If you accept this premise, then each encounter reflects back to you an opportunity to explore your relationship to yourself and to learn. Assume for a moment that the qualities you admire in others—their strengths, abilities, and positive attributes—are really characteristics you have already embraced within yourself. You can therefore allow them to illuminate more clearly your own feelings of self-worth.

Conversely, you can view the people you judge negatively as gifts, presented to show you what you are not accepting about yourself. Imagine that every time you are angered, hurt, or irritated by another, you are actually being given the opportunity to heal past incidents of anger, hurt, or irritation. Perhaps viewing weakness in others is an opportunity to extend the loving arm of compassion to them; or it could be the perfect moment to heal the unconscious judgment you have secretly harbored against yourself.

When you approach life in this manner, those with whom you have the greatest grievances as well as those you admire and love can be seen as mirrors, guiding you to discover parts of yourself that you reject and to embrace your greatest qualities.

To shift your perspective radically from judgment of other/outer to a lifelong exploration of self/inner is the challenge of Rule Seven. Your task is to assess all the decisions, judgments, and projections you make onto others and to begin to view them as clues to how you can heal yourself and become whole.

The lessons offered by Rule Seven include tolerance, clarity, healing, and support. As we learn these lessons, we take a vital step toward shifting our perspective from others to ourselves.

TOLERANCE

"Everything that irritates us about others can lead us to an understanding of ourselves."

Carl Jung

In Rule One, you learned the lesson of acceptance, in which you learned to embrace all parts of yourself. Tolerance is the outward extension of acceptance; it is when you learn to embrace all parts of others and allow them to be and express themselves fully as the unique humans that they are. You will need to learn tolerance in order to coexist peacefully with others. Tolerance quiets the inner critic that chatters in your mind so that you can apply the old adage, "live and let live."

When I was sixteen years old, I remember walking down Fifty-seventh Street in New York City and being suddenly aware, for the first time, of a voice in my head talking to me. It sounded like a running commentary on everyone within my field of vision. I heard it broadcasting impressions incessantly, and the majority were far from kind. I realized that I could—and did—find fault with every single person I passed. The next thought that came to me was, "Isn't that amazing, I must be the only perfect person in the universe, since everyone else apparently has something wrong with him."

Once I realized how ridiculous this sounded, it dawned on me that perhaps my judgments of all these people on the street were reflections of myself as opposed to some objective reality. I began to understand that what I was seeing about each of them said more about me than it said about each of them. I also realized that perhaps I was judging everyone else harshly as a way to feel good about myself. By perceiving them as too fat, short, or strangely dressed, I was by comparison thinner, taller, and more stylish. In my mind, my intolerance of them rendered me superior.

Some part of me knew that judging others is a

way of covering up feelings of insufficiency and insecurity. I decided to examine each judgment I heard in my head and think of it as a mirror allowing me to glimpse some hidden part of myself. I discovered that there were very few people whom I viewed as "acceptable," and the majority of them were very similar to me. Since I rarely allowed myself to relate to anyone who was not exactly like me, I had put myself into an isolated box. From that day on, I used every judgment as a gift to learn more about myself.

Making this shift meant that I had to give up judging the world. Giving up my righteous intolerance meant that I could no longer deem myself automatically superior to anyone, and the result was that I needed to take a good look at my own flaws.

I recently had a business lunch with a man who displayed objectionable table manners. My first reaction was to judge him as offensive and his table manners as disgusting. When I noticed that I was judging him, I stopped and asked myself what I was feeling. I discovered that I was embarrassed to be seen with someone who was chewing with his mouth open and loudly blowing his nose into his linen napkin. I was astonished to find how much I cared about how the other people in the restaurant perceived me. I consciously had to shift from perceiving the situation as being about him to it being about me and my embarrassment. This allowed me to use this man's actions as a mirror with which to see my own insecurities about being seen with a person who was less than perfect, and how that reflected on me.

The ultimate goal of making such a shift in perception and learning tolerance is to get to the moment of saying, "So what if this person is..." and thereby taking your power back. If I had allowed my lunch partner to continue to disgust me, I would have given all my power to him. I would have allowed his actions to dictate my feelings. By recognizing that my judgment of him had everything to do with me, I neutralized the effect his manners had on me and took back my power.

Whenever you find yourself intolerant of someone, ask yourself, "What is the feeling underneath this judgment that I don't want to feel?" It might be discomfort, embarrassment, insecurity, anxiety, or some other feeling of diminishment that the person is evoking in you. Focus on actually feeling that feeling so that your intolerance can evaporate, and you can embrace both your own emotions and the actions or behavior of the person you are judging.

Remember that your judgment of someone will not serve as a protective shield against you becoming like him. Just because I judged my lunch partner as offensive does not *prevent* me from ever looking or acting like him, just as extending tolerance to him would not *cause* me to suddenly begin chewing my food with my mouth open. As tough and rigid as judgment and intolerance may be, it can never protect you from anything but love.

CLARITY

"Once in a while you get shown the light in the strangest of places if you look at it right."

Jerry Garcia

Clarity is the state of seeing clearly. You achieve clarity in those moments of startling insight when you are able to shift your perspective by viewing a situation in a new light. I like to think of clarity as the result of applying Windex to your soul. As you begin to view others as mirrors of yourself, it is as if you move into a new reality in which you experience life with astonishing crystal vision. You learn the lesson of clarity in the exact moments that you accomplish this perspective shift.

I achieved a moment of clarity that day when I was sixteen, when I suddenly tuned in to the running commentator voice inside my head. I saw a woman named Elaine learn clarity the moment she realized that all her anger directed at her disorganized husband was really anger at herself for embodying that very same quality. A friend of mine experienced it when she allowed herself to see that her pattern of harshly judging men was her own fear of commitment projected outward. You may learn clarity in any random moment of your life, as soon as you open your inner eyes to what your judgments of others are saying about you.

The best way to learn clarity is to identify those times when you are *not* experiencing it; the moments of fogginess can be clues that the lesson of clarity is being presented. When you are focused on your judgments of others, you are not using them as mirrors, and hence are stuck in the fog. When you are focused on the way someone else has behaved, you are in the fog. In essence, whenever you are disassociated from what the situation is saying about you and your perceptions, and focused instead on what it is saying about the other person, you are in the fog.

In those moments, clarity can be achieved simply by shifting perspective from other/outer to self/inner. Those are the moments to pause and ask yourself what you are feeling and through what personal lens you are viewing the circumstance. The moment you hold up the mirror, you begin to approach clarity.

HEALING

"Healing is a matter of time, but it is sometimes also a matter of opportunity."

Hippocrates

Healing is restoration to a state of wholeness and well-being. While healing is generally thought of in physical terms, it is no less essential in the emotional and spiritual realm. Healing is a lifelong process that endeavors to unearth the issues clouding your soul and to repair the metaphorical holes in your heart.

All people have healing as a required lesson at some point in their lives. Even those who appear to have perfect lives, devoid of issues, will not be able to bypass this lesson. Life presents too many obstacles and tests for anyone to sail through completely unscathed. Fortunately, we live in a culture that is tuned in to the importance of healing, so a wide range of resources are available. Whatever method you choose is irrelevant; what is important is that you take the time to nurture yourself toward wholeness.

The journey toward wholeness can be expedited if you are willing to use your outer experiences as tools to heal your own inner wounds. Every negative experience is a chance to heal something within yourself. A male friend once confided in me that he was suffering from impotence. He was deeply ashamed about this and filled with self-loathing. He knew his impotence resulted from feelings of unworthiness stemming from when his old girl-friend left him abruptly for another man, yet he was unable to repair his self-esteem.

Eventually, my friend met a wonderful woman named Andrea who loved him unconditionally. It took many months for my friend to finally allow Andrea's unconditional acceptance of him to reflect its healing properties onto his own damaged image of himself. He gradually allowed her to act as a mir-ror for his own self-acceptance and, through her love, learn to love himself again. Happily, his impo-tence vanished along with his other negative feelings.

It is entirely possible that other people's positive perceptions of us can heal any damage in our self-esteem. But healing through mirroring can occur another way, as well. We can learn to heal past wounds the moment they are triggered in the present moment. This is done by dealing with the feelings that surface in certain difficult situations once and for all. The people who act as mirrors in the present can give you the gift of healing wounds from the past.

Stephanie, one of my clients, wanted to leave her job at a publishing house to go into business for herself as a freelance editor. However, she and her boss/mentor had been locked in a dysfunctional working relationship for nearly seven years, and she was having a difficult time separating from him. He treated her like a child, rarely allowing her to make any decisions on her own without consulting him first and keeping her on an extremely short leash. Whenever Stephanie protested or tried to assert her independence, her boss would make her feel guilty by saying he had invested many years in her and that she owed him her career.

When Stephanie came to me, she was feeling frustrated, beaten down, and incapable of breaking free from this situation. She expressed deep disdain for her boss, yet contradicted her venomous remarks with loving, fatherly stories about him. It was clear to me that Stephanie had some parent/child healing to do and that this situation was a perfect opportunity to mirror back to her what she needed.

When I asked Stephanie if this situation reminded her of anything or anyone, she immediately told me a story from when she was twenty-one years old. She was officially leaving home for the first time, moving out of her parents' house and in with her long-term boyfriend. Her mother took Stephanie's leaving home as a personal betrayal, and verbally attacked Stephanie the night before she moved out. Sitting in her room amidst her packed bags late that night, Stephanie looked up and saw her mother swooping down the hallway toward her, her robe flying out behind her like a witch's cape. When her mother reached her, she hissed at Stephanie, "What you are doing is selfish. Just plain selfish. How dare you leave like this?" Stephanie cowered, and snuck out of the house early the next morning.

Stephanie and I agreed that the situation with her boss was mirroring an old wound of guilt and recollections of not being able to stand up for herself. We both knew she was being given an opportunity to heal this wound by leaving the right way this time, with her dignity and with honor. After many rehearsals, Stephanie eloquently, graciously, and with unshakable confidence told her boss she was leaving to further her own growth. Thus, the old wound in her psyche was healed.

What wounds do you carry that need to be healed?

SUPPORT

"There are two ways of spreading light: to be the candle or the mirror that reflects it."

Edith Wharton

Support is holding up from underneath. You support someone when you willingly step forward to strengthen, energize, and help her through a challenging time. Yet the great irony is that when you support others, you are also, in fact, supporting yourself. When you withhold support from others, it is usually an indicator that you are also withholding support from yourself.

When I train people to become facilitators of my workshops, the primary thing I teach them is to be aware of how much their support of the individual workshop participants mirrors their own issues. If a facilitator is having difficulty supporting a participant who is expressing rage, it is a good sign that he or she is not supporting his or her own tolerance of or personal tendency toward rage. If the facilitator cannot support someone developing her sense of inner power, then it is the facilitator's own rejection of his or her own inner power that is getting in the way. This is not unlike the training of psychoanalysts, in which they use their own reactions to patients as mirrors in which the patients can view themselves.

We are most often called upon to support others in friendship. One of my facilitators, Donna, told me a story recently that clearly illustrates the magic of support and its potential as an emotional mirror. Several years ago, Donna had been feeling very depressed. She had just broken up with her boyfriend of two years, and she was having a very difficult time accepting the loss. She had been laid up with a knee injury for several days, and the time alone at home certainly was not helping. Her misery was only compounded by her frustration at herself for not being able to "pull it together" and stop crying all the time.

Early one morning, Donna received a phone call with some terrible news: her best friend's brother had been killed in a car accident. Donna had known this friend, Mary Ann, and her brother nearly her entire life, and the news was devastating. However, Donna quickly pulled herself together, got in the car, and drove to her friend's house to be there with her.

Over the course of the next few days, amidst the haze of the funeral and hundreds of visitors, Donna was 100 percent present for Mary Ann. She held her close while she cried endless tears, sat by her side as the waves of grief washed over her friend, and slept on the floor next to Mary Ann's bed to make sure she did not wake up alone in the middle of the night. During that time she hardly felt any pain in her knee at all and none of the depression she had been experiencing.

Several weeks later, when life began to return to normal, Donna realized that the level of support she had given Mary Ann far exceeded any support she had offered herself during her dark time. She was able to use the support she had given her friend as a mirror for the support she had been withholding from herself. She realized that her own tears required as much attention and nurturing from her as anyone else's, and that if she could give it to another, she must be able to also give it to herself.

When you find yourself unable to support

someone else, look within and see if perhaps there is something within yourself that you are not supporting. Conversely, when you give complete support to others, it will mirror those places within you that require the same level of attention.

WHAT YOU MAKE OF YOUR LIFE IS UP TO YOU

You have all the tools and resources you need. What you do with them is up to you.

Every person creates his or her own reality. Authorship of your life is one of your absolute rights; yet so often people deny that they have the ability to script the life they desire. They often use the excuse that they cannot do what they want to do or get what they desire in life because they lack the resources to do it. They look past the fundamental truth that it is not our external resources that determine our success or failure, but rather our own belief in ourselves and our willingness to create a life according to our highest aspirations.

You can either engage in the blame game, making frequent use of the statement, "I couldn't because . . . ," or you can take control of your life and shape it as you would like. You can either let your circumstances, be they your physical appearance, your financial condition, or your family origins, dictate what happens to you, or you can transcend your perceived limitations and make extraordinary things happen. The "yeah, buts..." do not produce results—they just reinforce the delusion of inability. Argue for your limitations and eventually the universe will agree with you and respond accordingly.

Joseph Cambell once said, "The world is a match for you, and you are a match for the world." By this he meant that when you fully recognize your challenges, your gifts, and your individual reality, and you accept the life path they represent, the world provides whatever you need to succeed. You, in turn, will discover how you can make your greatest contribution to the world. When you claim authorship of your life story, the world responds, and genius ignites.

Clearly, the challenge of Rule Eight is to create and own your own reality. The first moment you are able to do this is an awakening of sorts, since it means the demise of your unconscious life. I remember vividly the time in my life when this occurred. It was after I had received my three messages about what I was supposed to do with my life. Much to my surprise, rather than feeling relieved or inspired, I felt depressed. After crying for what seemed like days, with hardly any idea why, I came to realize that the phase of my life in which I could float in the murky swamp of "I don't know" was coming to an end. Once I received the three messages and knew what my purpose was, I had moved out of the safety zone of not knowing, otherwise known as "childhood," into the reality of the adult world. I knew that once I began consciously to own my life, it would be nearly impossible to sink back into oblivion. I wept tears of loss, for I had passed through a tunnel of maturity and left my unconscious life behind. Though sad, I was now ready to take command of my life.

When you begin to live your life understanding that what you make of it is up to you, you are able to design it according to your authentic choices and desires. You will learn lessons with this Rule, such as responsibility, release, courage, power, and adventure, that will lead you to the life you were meant to live. These lessons provide you with the essential tools you need in order to take command of your life.

RESPONSIBILITY

"We have to accept the consequences of every deed, word, and thought throughout our lifetime."

Elisabeth Kübler-Ross

To take responsibility means you admit your accountability and acknowledge your influence and role in the circumstances in which you find yourself. It means you are answerable for your behavior and you fully accept any consequences created by your actions.

Responsibility is not blame, however, and understanding the difference between the two is crucial to learning this lesson. Blame is associated with fault, whereas responsibility denotes authorship. Blame carries guilt and negative feelings; responsibility brings the relief of not having to dodge the full truth anymore and releases that guilt. Blame implies fault; responsibility implies ownership. Blame is stagnant; responsibility propels you forward and onward to your greater good.

Responsibility comes with certain rewards, but it is a lesson that is often hard-earned. I once had a woman named Mary in my workshop whose story of personal responsibility has always inspired me. Mary was born in Cuba and moved to Miami with her family when she was two years old. They lived in terrible poverty in a dangerous part of the city, where crime and drugs were part of everyday life. Mary was determined, however, even at the young age of eight, to make something of her life other than follow the expected route of becoming a maid, or a cashier at the supermarket. So she got herself to school each and every day, sometimes having to step over drunks passed out in the doorway, just so she could get an education and give herself a better life.

Mary eventually left Miami, obtained a good education, and fostered her natural music ability. She knew it was up to her to create her own life, regardless of what hand she had been dealt. She is now one of the most well-known Latina studio singers, and her voice can be heard in countless national commercials. Mary could have given in to the life she was born into, or remained mired in blaming her parents and culture for her circumstances. She could have allowed a refusal to take responsibility for a situation—*even though she was not to blame for it*—to overshadow her desire. Instead, however, Mary took responsibility for herself and created a life of which she can be proud.

As a parent, I find myself trying to teach my daughter, Jennifer, small lessons of responsibility every day. I want Jennifer to grow up to be the kind of person who does what she says she will do, who understands the obligations that go along with privileges, and who takes ownership of her role in whatever circumstances she finds herself. I know I have a small window of time in which to impress upon her the importance of responsibility before she sets out into the world on her own.

Responsibility is a major lesson of adulthood. If you still haven't learned the lesson of responsibility, it's not too late. Remember, life will provide you with plenty of opportunities to get it right.

RELEASE

"Learn to let go. That is the key to happiness."

The Buddha

Release is simply the act of letting go. In every situation, you can either take responsibility and attempt to cause things to happen, or you can let go. Neither option is better or worse. Every situation is different, and only you will know what is the right thing to do in each case. There are times when you will need to take responsibility for the progression of a relationship, and times you will need to just let go and walk away, just as there are times you need to fight with your boss for what you believe and other times when you need to release the situation to save your energy for more important battles. You learn the lesson of release when you begin to choose it as a conscious act rather than as a passive means to hide from responsibility.

There will be times in your life when you will

need to let go of certain self-beliefs that hold you back from creating your own reality. A woman in one of my workshops named Nancy suffered from a lack of self-esteem that was limiting her ability to create the life she wanted to live. She never felt that she deserved the best of anything, and as a result, she always settled for "good enough." Nancy traced this belief back to her childhood in Brazil, in which she was always treated as inferior to her older sister. Nancy's mother always introduced her as "the second child," which created a belief in Nancy's mind that she would always be second best. Her entire wardrobe was secondhand, and all her toys had already been enjoyed by her sister. Nancy needed to release this belief so that she could enable herself to make appropriate and deserved demands in her adult life.

Another emotion that often lurks in people's minds is anger. They cling to their anger toward their parents for the way they were raised, or toward their spouse for disappointing them, or toward fate for presenting them with injustices. This anger can fester in their unconscious minds, blocking the flow of their natural power to create their lives. They focus so intently on their negative feelings that they are blind to the power of forgiveness and release.

Sometimes negative memories can clutter your mind and take up the space needed in order to imagine and create a life based on what you want. It is unfortunate that "bad" things happen, but clinging to the psychic debris left behind can do even more damage than the actual event. People are able to overcome and release even the most heinous of experiences if they are willing. The human heart is remarkably resilient, and you will need to trust yours in order to release the memories that stagnate you.

Other times you will need to let go of situations, like a toxic relationship or a degrading job, so that you can create a better reality for yourself. I remember consulting a few years ago with a couple who were trapped in the sticky web of a toxic relationship. Eric and Sarah were practically torturing each other with criticism, anger, and inconsiderate behavior. When I asked them why they stayed together in light of their mutual unhappiness, neither could really produce a logical answer. As we talked about their relationship, both Eric and Sarah began to see that by clinging to what was obviously an impossible situation, they could both avoid progressing with their independent lives. They both admitted a fear of having to create a new reality for themselves. This admission created enough awareness for the need to release that union to allow them to do so.

Regardless of what emotion or belief you have lingering in your unconscious that prevents you from creating your own reality, you can learn to release it by remembering two lessons you already learned: awareness and willingness. Once you become aware of what stands in your way and become willing to release it, you signal the universe that you are ready to manifest the life you were meant to live.

COURAGE

"Courage is the price life exacts for granting peace."
Amelia Earhart

Courage is finding the inner strength and bravery required when confronting danger, difficulty, or opposition. Courage is the energy current behind all great actions and the spark that ignites the initial baby steps of growth. It resides deep within each of us, ready to be accessed in those moments when you need to forge ahead or break through seemingly insurmountable barriers. It is the intangible force that propels you forward on your journey.

It takes courage to embrace the idea that what you make of your life is up to you and to actually *do* what you need to do. You can learn how to access your courage by digging down deep inside and tapping into whatever spiritual connection sustains you. What inspires you to action? For some it is a belief in a higher power, for some it can be meditation or inspiring music, and for others perhaps great literature or spiritual passages. Regardless of what your connection is to the divine source, cultivate it well, for you will need to call upon it in those moments when you require courage.

There are, of course, those times when you may be unable to locate that reservoir of courage stored inside you. That is when you will need to draw on the support of loved ones around you. You can borrow the courage you need from other people who believe in you strongly to get you through the phases of temporary amnesia when you forget your own abilities and tenacity.

Courage is learned in the moment that you take a leap of faith and take action. I remember learning to dive as a child. For weeks, I stood at the tip of the diving board at our local pool, trying to work up the courage to plunge headfirst into the water below. My father stood at the bottom of the ladder three Saturdays in a row, offering encouragement. He demonstrated over and over how to do it, but I still felt afraid. The fear was nameless, since I was pretty sure I would not injure myself, and failure wasn't really a concern. I suppose I was simply afraid in the way that humans often are when they stand poised to jump, metaphorically or literally, into the unknown.

Finally, the day came when I realized that I could psych myself up all I wanted, and receive endless support from my father, but ultimately I would have to take a deep breath and just *go*. I climbed the ladder one more time, stood at the now-familiar edge of that board, said a little prayer, and dove. It was not a perfect dive, but it was a dive nonetheless. No blaring trumpets heralded the glory of my accomplishment, but it was in that moment that I learned the valuable lesson of courage that would remain with me the rest of my life.

What fears stand in your way? Bring them to light so you can loosen their hold over you. Fears, real or imagined, only impede you. Banish them so that you may learn the lesson of courage and create the life you desire.

POWER

"There isn't a person anywhere who isn't capable of doing more than he thinks he can."

Henry Ford

Power means demonstrating your ability to manifest reality. Within each of us lies a power center, and we learn to call upon this power as we set out to design our lives according to our will. Power is a natural state of being—it is a force to which we are all entitled and to which we all have unlimited access.

It is not necessary to search for your inner power, since it is already within you. It is something you were given the moment you were born, as essential to your survival as the ability to breathe. Your power is what propels you forward day after day, what sustains you in dark moments, what gives you the ability to do whatever you feel driven to do. It glows within you like a light, beamed outward into the world as needed.

In 1983, I started a nonprofit business that trained young adults aged eighteen to twenty-five to manage households overseas. I was extremely passionate about this program and dedicated to making it succeed. Our lawyer at the time was a gruff, distinguished older man named Marcus who, at 6 foot 4 inches, towered over me and was very intimidating. He insisted that we would never get the visas we needed to authorize foreigners to live in the United States for one year and learn in a domestic setting. Even as we stood in the hallway waiting to go in for our interview with the Immigration and Naturalization Service (INS), Marcus dismissed my passion and told me that I was wasting my time even applying for the visas.

In that moment, I knew I needed to call on my own inner strength in order to succeed on my mission. I took a deep breath, reminded myself that I could succeed at anything I set my mind to, and stood up to this imposing lawyer. I told Marcus that I had every confidence that we would get the visas and that I expected his full support. He and I then went before the INS, and much to my satisfaction and his shock, I stood my ground and answered all their questions flawlessly. I think even Marcus was secretly delighted when the INS approved my application.

There may be times, however, when you have difficulty seeing that light within you. You may experience "power leaks" that rob you of your ability to manifest reality. In those times, you will need to identify what is robbing you of your power and patch the leaks.

Power leaks come in many forms: intimidation, discouragement and disappointment, setbacks, rejection, or loss, just to name a few. A leak is sprung whenever your inner resiliency is damaged or your feelings of self-worth are diminished. The best way to patch these leaks is to look back at your earlier successes as a way to remind yourself of what you are capable of. Do things that let you experience your power—even little things like hanging a picture or programming your VCR—to gradually seal the leaks and rebuild your confidence.

You may need to patch leaks in your power many times throughout your life, but once you groove an easy path back to the power source within you and live from within it, you will never again question the idea that what you make of your life is entirely up to you.

ADVENTURE

"Life is either a daring adventure or nothing at all."

Helen Keller

Your life has the potential to be a wondrous journey, filled with exciting moments and astonishing experiences. It can be a thrilling ride if you are open to exploring all that is available to you. Adventure is the result of your willingness to live life with a spirit of enthusiasm.

An adventure is any experience that takes you beyond your comfort level. Adventures are what make your blood race and your heart beat with anticipation as you expand beyond your perceived limitations as a human. They expand your horizons and take you into new and exciting worlds. When you feel the aliveness of experimenting with new options and taking risks, you learn the value of adventure in your life.

Since what you make of your life is up to you, you can either create a life filled with miraculous adventures or stay huddled and safe, never experiencing the joyful rush of journeying outside your world with boldness and abandon. A life devoid of adventure may be secure, but it is one that lacks texture and color. If you never venture forth, you can never expand and grow.

A sense of adventure is inherent in young children. We are all born with an innate sense of wonder that propels us to explore. Most children are naturally curious and experimental, ready to try anything. They are not held back by fears of societal disapproval or failure. As they grow up, however, the world imposes its fears and limitations upon them, and very often this sense of adventure is buried beneath years of admonishments like "Don't touch!" and "Behave!" The spark of adventure gets dimmed as they learn to become responsible, mature adults.

This childlike sense of wonder must be reignited so that you can remember the thrill of discovering new worlds. This spark usually shows up as bold impulses that you may dismiss as silly or imprudent, like a sudden urge to try windsurfing or a desire to travel to Alaska. As you reconnect to this spark and honor it, however, you open the door to wonderful experiences and magical connections. You begin to take bigger and bolder steps toward living your dreams.

There was a time in my life that I was unwilling to heed that spark. I focused all my energy on being responsible and disciplined, neglecting the basic human need to explore and expand. Eventually, my life began to look so dull that I forced myself to snap out of my rigidity and reembrace my long-lost sense of adventure. I missed being the person who was open to discovering new sensations, and who took bold risks. I promised myself back then that I would always make my best effort to remain conscious to that inner spark so that I never missed out on a chance to expand. Since that time, I have been blessed with a miraculous life, filled with incredible journeys and experiences that might have otherwise escaped me if I had not woken up.

During my last trip to New York, I visited Riverside Church on the Upper West Side of Manhattan. It was a clear, beautiful night in December, and I suddenly felt the impulse to go up to the top of the church so I could see the magnificent view of the city. I knew from my past experiences that that impulse was a signal that my sense of adventure was leading me toward something wonderful. Despite a mild fear of heights, I climbed what seemed like a thousand steps to the top.

As I had suspected, the view was magnificent. The twinkling lights below glittered like a million stars, reflected in the river like jewels. As I breathed in the cold night air, I experienced one of those moments of perfect joy. I felt a wave of gratitude that I had honored my sense of adventure and given myself the gift of this experience.

Think back to the adventures you have had in your lifetime. Those moments in which you took a leap of faith and expanded beyond your comfort zone are precious gifts, as they can remind you of the joy that is available to you when you embrace life with exuberance. These moments can be turning points in your personal history and inspire you to create new realities for yourself whenever you choose.

Imagine yourself at ninety years old, looking back on your life. What do you want to see? Whenever I think about that, I remember my friend in college who always used to say, "You only regret that which you don't do." I do not want to look back at a life filled with regrets. What I want to see is a life filled with magical moments inspired by adventure like the one I experienced on the roof of that church. Could you use more adventure in your life? If so, follow the words of Goethe:

> *"Whatever you can do, or dream you can, begin it.*
> *Boldness has genius, power, and magic in it."*

ALL YOUR ANSWERS LIE INSIDE OF YOU

All you need to do is look, listen, and trust.

All the answers you are looking for are already within your grasp; all you need to do is look inside, listen, and trust yourself. There is no outside source of wisdom that can give you the answers to any of your innermost questions; you alone are your wisest teacher. Deep inside, you already know all you need to know.

We all possess spiritual DNA, which is the inner wisdom that resides within us and transmits messages about our life path. These messages are signals or directives from your inner source of intuition that guide you toward and through your authentic life. Messages are like illuminated stepping stones along your path that point to the actions you need to take in order to continue your process of growth.

They flash and pop in your innermost mind, offering directions and clues, and providing you with all the answers you need.

These powerful hints are available to you at any time and can come in a variety of forms. They can come as a "little voice" in your head, or as an intuitive flash. They can arrive in a letter or a phone call or printed on the inside flap of a box of tea. They can sound like a whisper—like Kevin Costner's message in the movie *Field of Dreams* of "If you build it, they will come"—or like a distant chime. A clue that something is truly a message: It just doesn't go away, no matter how hard you try to ignore it. It reappears until you are willing to listen and honor it.

Even if you are not open to them, your true messages have a way of finding you no matter where you hide. If you shut the door, they come in the window. Seal the window and they will come down the chimney. As the saying goes, "What you resist, persists." Your truth will find you no matter where you hide. Ignoring your inner voice or closing yourself off to your inner truth only invites it to show up in other, more negative, ways, such as depression, addictive behaviors, or simply discontent. The sooner you open to your truth, the quicker and farther you can advance along your path. Life flows more smoothly when we heed our inner messages.

Many years ago, when I was living in Boston, I went to dinner with several members of my staff.

Three of us had arrived early and were waiting for the remaining four people to show up, and since it was a cold, snowy December night, we went inside to wait for them. They were quite late, and since these were very responsible people, I was puzzled as to where they were.

Nearly an hour later, they still had not arrived. I kept wondering what had happened to them. Suddenly I became aware of a small voice in my head, buzzing like an annoying bee, that said, "Go stand on the corner." Now, I was seven months pregnant at that time, and between my large size and the frigid temperature, I had no intention whatsoever of going outside to stand on the corner. I shooed the message away and continued with my conversation.

However, like all true messages, this one simply would not vanish at my command. I kept hearing the message, "Go stand on the corner." Finally, more out of annoyance than anything else, I stood up, wrapped my coat around my huge circumference and excused myself for a moment to—yes, you guessed it—go stand on the corner. I looked and felt ridiculous.

Within one minute of my arriving on the corner, the remaining members of my staff pulled up in their car. They were thrilled to see me, as they had been driving around lost for close to an hour. When they asked me why I happened to be standing out on that corner just as they drove by, I just smiled, rolled my eyes, and replied, "Don't ask." That night I promised myself I would always pay attention to my messages to the best of my ability, no matter how ridiculous they might sound. I knew then that they were my link to all the knowledge already stored within me.

It makes no difference whether your messages show up in ridiculous-sounding mandates like the one I just described or in more direct forms. A recurring message to take your dog to the park is no less important or valid than a message to leave your job at a big corporation and start your own shop. Perhaps the first message is a result of your sensing that you need to be in the outdoors more often for the sake of your health, which is just as important as where you earn your living. All messages, silly or not, are powerful truth guides that provide you with direct access to your inner knowing.

If you listen carefully, you can tune into the frequency that transmits this valuable information to you. The challenge of Rule Nine is to tune in and honor the messages and answers you receive from your spiritual blueprint. Since your mind chatters constantly, it is often difficult to hear the messages that contain the true answers. When you do hear them, however, they may sound bizarre to you if you are out of touch with your true feelings. A thirty-five-year-old highly regarded art dealer may dismiss the answer she receives from within as to why she feels alienated and unfulfilled if that answer tells her she needs to fulfill her lifelong dream of going to medical school to become a psychiatrist. Messages that do not coincide with your agenda are easy to dismiss, but still difficult to ignore.

By tuning in to your messages, however, you learn what you truly need. When you choose to honor these answers, you can live a life based on your authentic inner knowing and feelings, thus getting away from feeling "the impostor syndrome." Perhaps that art dealer really would be happier starting her life over and becoming a doctor. Only she and her inner guide can be sure.

To tune in and honor your inner knowing, you need to learn the lessons of listening, trust, and inspiration. These lessons will lead you to a place within yourself, from which you can access all the answers you need about what will make your experience on Earth a rewarding one.

LISTENING

"Consciousness is nothing but awareness—the composite of all the things we pay attention to."

Deepak Chopra

Listening is actively focusing on what messages you are receiving, both verbally and nonverbally. Nowhere is the lesson of listening more important than when it comes to your inner knowing; what good is such divine knowledge if you don't tune in and hear it? You will learn the lesson of listening when you tune in to the messages your spiritual DNA is sending you, and to what you know is right for you.

There is an old joke about a religious man who had an unshakeable faith in God. He prayed every day and felt that if anything ever happened, the Lord would be there to take care of him.

One day it started to rain. The man's village flooded, and everyone hurried to escape. Some people came driving by his house in a car, urging him to come with them to safety.

His reply was, "The Lord will save me."

The rain continued to fall, until the water rose so high that the man needed to go up to the second floor of his house to stay dry. A boat came by, and the people on it urged him to climb aboard and go with them to safety.

Again, he responded, "Thank you kindly, but the Lord will save me."

The man soon needed to go up on the roof in order to avoid the rapidly rising water. A helicopter flew by and the pilot shouted down, "I'll toss you a line and we'll hoist you up."

For a third time, the man refused. "Bless you," he said to the pilot, "but the Lord will save me. Any minute, you'll see, the Lord will do something and I will be saved."

Within minutes the water level rose, washing the

man out to sea, where he drowned. He went to heaven, and when the Lord was reviewing the new arrivals, he was surprised to see the religious man.

"You're not supposed to be here!" said the Lord. "It's not your time. What are you doing here?"

The man said to the Lord, "I believed in You. I believed that You would save me. I waited and waited, and You never came. What happened?"

The Lord replied, "I sent you a car, a boat, and a helicopter. What more do you want?"

The point is that we need to listen closely to hear our messages, as they do not always sound or look the way we think they will. You need to be tuned in to pick up their frequency, or else you might miss some important clues being generated from your spiritual center.

TRUST

"Trust thyself; every heart vibrates to that iron string."

Ralph Waldo Emerson

Once you learn to listen to your messages, you then move to the next, deeper level of growth: trusting those messages. You learn the lesson of trust when you take a leap of faith and believe that your inner knowing is guiding you toward your greater good. Trust is the attunement of your instincts to know who and what is in your best interest, so that you may rely absolutely on the validity of your messages.

The heart of my Inner Negotiation Workshop is encouraging participants to trust their messages. Very often this creates fear in them, as they cannot comprehend that it is safe within the confines of the workshop to act upon and trust whatever message they are receiving. Once they relax into it and trust, however, incredible things happen. I have seen a normally reserved corporate banker wailing away on an electric guitar. I have watched Sari, a model from New York, trust her message that she needed to let out a howl right then and there, even though she had no idea why. Howl she did, and *LOUDLY.* By trusting that message, Sari got in touch with a long-lost need within her to be out in nature. She kept her job in New York but now makes sure to spend adequate time out in the woods, where she feels connected and centered.

We are taught throughout our lives not to trust ourselves. Children are consistently told to do things their parents' way, "because they said so." The media trains us to look outside ourselves—in products, entertainment, or gurus—for the answers. Even most modern schooling does not encourage self-reliant thinking. We are bombarded with messages from every angle that tell us that we cannot trust our own inner directives.

During Emily's childhood, there were times when people told her that her feelings were inappropriate for a given situation. For example, on her twelfth birthday Emily was having a sad day and made no attempt to hide her feelings. Her mother reprimanded her with words like, "You should be happy at your own party. You should smile and have a wonderful day." Another time, the day Emily's grandmother passed away, Emily's mother scolded her for playing in the garden. "Stop all that laughter. Don't you know someone's died? You're supposed to be mourning."

At these and other times, Emily was criticized for being herself and expressing spontaneous feelings. Each time this happened, she felt confused, out of sync with events around her, and unable to trust her own emotions. As she grew to adulthood, she carried this self-doubt with her. With every decision she faced, she would ask other people's opinions before taking action. When someone asked her a question, she often had to answer, "I don't know," and then ask friends what they would say. Emily's major life lesson was to learn to trust her feelings, her intuition, and her choices.

At age thirty-two, Emily wanted to start a business creating and selling doll-making kits through mail order. She'd been sewing all her life, had made dozens of dolls for friends, and was excited about turning her hobby into a business.

But family and friends were afraid for Emily. The capital investment would be considerable, she had no business experience, and there were no guarantees that the doll kits would actually sell. As more friends expressed doubts, Emily began to waver. She started talking about returning to school for another degree instead. That's when a friend suggested to Emily that she see me.

After talking over her business idea and all the fears and doubts around it, I asked Emily, "Putting aside the practical considerations, and without regard for the outcome, if you could do anything in the world what would it be?"

Without hesitating a second, Emily answered, "Make my doll kits and sell them."

I sat back in my seat, looked at her with amazement, and said, "That was as clear as anything I have ever heard." Emily had even surprised herself with the clarity of her answer.

When I asked her what stood in the way of moving ahead, she confessed, "I've never done anything that my friends and family disapproved of."

There was silence in the room. "How does it feel to consider the possibility?"

"Scary!"

"It sounds as if this is about self-trust," I suggested. "Am I right in assuming that you need to really trust yourself to take this risk?"

She stared at the floor for a long time before answering. "You're right on target. I don't know if I have enough belief in myself to go forward with no one behind me."

I had opened a door and given Emily the choice

of walking through alone. She decided to go for it. Her business succeeded beyond her wildest dreams, and she did get the support of her family and friends once she demonstrated her commitment to herself.

As Emily's story illustrates, trusting your instincts and your messages is an essential step in your spiritual growth, as they are the road map for your path. They are what lead you to your lessons, and you must learn to trust them if you are to learn all that you need in order to fulfill your special purpose.

You can begin to learn to trust your messages by starting with the small ones. For example, tune in and trust the simple messages like "Call your mother," or "Buy that dress," as a way to build your confidence in your inner radar. Recalling times in the past that trusting your instincts led you to the right course of action will also help. Whenever I receive a message from my inner source that sounds preposterous, I remember my "Go stand on the corner" story and trust that I would only lead myself into circumstances that were for the highest good.

INSPIRATION

"In the midst of our daily lives, we must find the juice to nourish our creative souls."

Sark

Inspiration is the moment in which the spirit within is accessed and revealed. Inspiration dawns when something in your outer world sparks a flame within you and calls forth a message. It arrives to remind you that all your answers lie inside of you, and that you alone are the wisest wizard in your kingdom.

It is often easy to miss those moments until you learn to truly hear the inner "ding!" and give it the space to emerge into your consciousness. As you move toward honoring your inner knowing, you can more easily recognize those moments of inspiration—many of which can be life-transforming.

Spending time in nature can be a wonderful source of inspiration. The natural world has an energy to it that can put you in touch with the deepest parts of yourself. Thoreau spent two years alone in the woods so he could commune with nature and access the wisdom inside him. It was there that he wrote some of his most inspiring work—much of which contains timeless wisdom that is every bit as valid and true a century later. He discovered that all his answers lay inside him, just as yours lie inside you. Swim in the ocean, climb a tree, hike a mountain, or simply take a long walk in the woods. Do whatever activity calls to you that will draw you into the rhythm of nature and draw out your natural instincts.

The arts can be another miraculous source of inspiration. Beautiful poetry or literature can open your heart and soul so that you may allow your innate knowledge to flow forth. A glorious piece of music or a magnificent painting can also spark the divine place within you. Each masterpiece was created in a moment of inspiration that can lead you back to your own.

My friend Laura keeps an "inspiration box" on her dresser, in which she stores quotes written on scraps of paper and objects that inspire her. She has everything in there from a Chinese fortune that says "You are your own deepest fountain" to a sparkly blue marble given to her by her young son. Whenever she is searching for an answer to one of life's many questions or problems, she reaches into her inspiration box and draws out something to put her in touch with her own wisdom.

What would you put in your inspiration box?

YOU WILL FORGET ALL OF THIS AT BIRTH

You can remember it if you want by unraveling the double helix of inner knowing.

Y ou came into this world already knowing all of the information imparted by these Ten Rules. You simply forgot them somewhere along your journey from the spirit world to the physical one. Each lesson is like another stone along your life path, and as you travel and learn your lessons, some may look and feel familiar. When something resonates for you and you finally "get" one of the lessons, you are remembering what you originally knew. When you have an "aha!" moment, you are remembering. When you are still and at peace, you are remembering. Some call it planets aligning, some call it feeling at one with God, still others call it serenity; call it what you want, but know it is a moment of remembering.

Remembering and forgetting are the dance of consciousness. Remembering is the moment when you awaken to your truth. Forgetting is the temporary amnesia that sets in when your truth is occluded. When you feel stuck, you have forgotten your truth. When you cannot break through, you have forgotten. When you move too far away from your conscious awareness, you lose touch with the universal wisdom that is inherent in all humans.

We each have many cycles of remembering and forgetting in our lifetime. You may remember and know the universal truths where they apply to one area of your life, such as work, but forget them completely when it comes to love and romance.

You may remember them one day and forget them completely by nightfall. The Ten Rules for Being Human are here as guidelines to help you when you forget and remind you of everything you already know. They are not commandments, but rather universal truths that are the same for everyone. When you lose your way, simply call upon them, and the temporary amnesia will be dispelled like storm clouds burned off by the sun.

The challenge of Rule Ten is to remember your truth, again and again, and to create ways to find your way back when you forget. You do this by learning the advanced lessons of faith, wisdom, and ultimately, limitlessness. Mastering these takes you to a deeper level of consciousness and a far greater realm of spiritual expansion.

Remaining rooted in truth means giving up the bliss of ignorance. But living from within truth gives life luster. It is what brings you to your authentic self and makes life an astonishing and meaningful experience.

FAITH

"Faith is a gift of the spirit that allows the soul to remain attached to its own unfolding."

Thomas Moore

Have faith in yourself that you will remember your truth and the knowledge stored deep within your soul. There may be moments in which you cannot see your way clear to your truth—moments of darkness and uncertainty. Life can be difficult, and there may be times when you cannot make sense out of it or stay afloat. These are the moments that require faith.

Faith is the lone candle in the darkness when you feel jettisoned out into space, and the invisible net that lies beneath you when you feel as though you may stumble. It is what carries you through those patches of temporary amnesia. Faith is simply believing, without any tangible proof, that although the truth may seem eclipsed at times, it does not disappear forever. It simply lies dormant inside you until you reconnect with your innate wisdom.

Faith is what carried Maya, a thirty-eight-year-old mother of two, through the painful months after her divorce, when she could not recall how it felt to experience joy. It is what kept Sam, a wealthy entrepreneur, afloat after his factory—and entire life's investments—burned to the ground in an electrical fire. Faith sustained my friend Ellen during her period of fear and uncertainty when she relocated to Paris, thousands of miles away from her familiar home. All of these people relied on faith as a means of remembering their capability to experience wholeness during those times when wholeness seemed lost to them. It was faith that helped them recall the wisdom stored in their souls.

There are many ways to restore your faith during the dark moments, when the light appears too dim to see and the truth seems too hazy to recall. By surrounding yourself with people who know your personal truth and who are familiar with your authentic self, you can keep yourself rooted to your truth. You can touch base with these people and ask them to remind you of the truth in your moments of temporary amnesia. Thea Alexander refers to these people as "personal evolution tutors." These tutors can provide you with the sparks of recognition you need at those times when your faith is weak.

My personal evolution tutor is my sister and soulmate Lynn, who keeps me on track. When I was in graduate school years ago, I nearly gave up many times because of all the pressure and endless work.

In my darkest moments, when I could not recognize why I was doing this to myself, Lynn reminded me how much I really did want to complete that degree. My temporary amnesia almost allowed me to abort the learning process and to sabotage a dream I had formulated when I was in my right and truthful mind. Lynn, as my personal evolution tutor, reconnected me with my choice by acting as the link to my inner truth.

Another way to keep your faith alive is through touchstones. In your enlightened moments, collect things that connect you to your source. They can be symbols, or objects, or bits of writing or quotes, or anything that brings you back to the place within you that is connected to the universal spirit. In your moments of forgetting, surround yourself with them to remind you of who you are and what you are capable of.

Faith can also be reignited by engaging in any activity that centers you. For some it is prayer, for others breathing, reading, meditating, jogging, drawing, or playing with the dog. These activities can act as mechanisms to pluck you out of your amnesia. What gives you spiritual energy? What acts as your life preserver? What is the motion that will pull you up when you are sinking? Spend some time while you are awake and conscious figuring out what life preserver you can hold on to to keep you above whatever threatens to drag you down.

These are only a few suggestions. You alone know what will help you remember and reconnect with your essence. Find it and treasure it close to your heart to draw upon in those moments when you stray too far from your truth.

WISDOM

"We don't receive wisdom; we must discover it for ourselves after a journey that no one can take for us or spare us."

Marcel Proust

The ultimate destination of your life path is wisdom. Wisdom is the highest and deepest degree of knowledge, insight, and understanding. It provides you with the broadest perspective on life, its purpose, and the lessons you learn throughout your lifetime. When you find your wisdom, you are living in the light.

Wisdom is not a state to be achieved, but rather a state to be recalled. You arrived on this planet fully equipped with the boundless wisdom inherent in all humans; you only need to access that place within you that connects you to the infinite divine source in order to remember it. You are every bit as wise as the Buddha, Aristotle, or Confucious—they have simply accessed places inside themselves where perhaps you have not yet journeyed.

Wisdom is not intelligence. It has nothing to do

with the level of your IQ or how well you did in school. Rather, wisdom is the highest level of emotional, spiritual, and mental evolution, at which you value intuition as much as information, willingness as much as ability, and inspiration as much as knowledge. It is where you synergize your deepest understanding with your everyday actions.

The most direct path to your wisdom is paved with your life's lessons. By learning the lessons presented to you every day, you continually bring yourself closer to aligning with what Emerson called "the oversoul" and Carl Jung called "the collective unconscious." These are the universal forces that tie us all together and link each of us to the bottomless source of wisdom. It is quite simple: learn your lessons so that you may find your link to that source and remember your wisdom.

The true beauty of wisdom is that once you recall it, you will then be inspired to pass it along. You will recall the lesson of abundance and know that there is no lack or limit to wisdom. It is like love; the more you give away, the more you get back. Your capacity for wisdom increases each time you share it with another. Those who are celebrated for their wisdom are those who have shared it freely to help others grow.

Elisabeth Kübler-Ross is one who used her wisdom to help millions of people cope with the process of dying. By coupling her wisdom with compassion, she has raised others to her level of understanding and allowed them to see that how we die is as important as how we live.

It is not every day that we encounter people who we would label as wise. A grandparent, teacher, mentor, someone who emanates a way of looking at life with a broad perspective—for some, way beyond their years. You know someone like this. It may be someone close to you, or someone famous like Mother Teresa, the Dalai Lama, Albert Schweitzer, or Jonas Salk. I was fortunate to know Willis Harman, the president of the Institute of Noetic Sciences, who for me, possessed this type of wisdom.

When I interacted with him, I felt as if we took a mental helicopter trip above the earth to address conditions below. I felt blessed to be in his presence. I was inspired when he shared his points of view with me. His absence of personal agenda, his complete lack of need or want and his freedom from dependance upon material possessions gave him incredible power. His reflections gave pause from the daily momentum of life. He wrote, ". . . we are likely to find ourselves involved in a self-transformation that leads to ultimate trust in the deep Self and in 'inner knowing,' bringing to awareness the deep sense of purpose and the source of wisdom and direction to be found there, confirming the intention to find our life work and do it. . . ." It was refreshing to bask in his philosophical musings and stretch into the shoes of a reality that I could not yet fill. I am continually grateful for my relationship with him, because through him I experienced those principles to which I aspire.

Think of the person in your life who gave you a peek at wisdom. Ask yourself what attributes you noticed. Then see what you want to emulate within yourself. You will gain a bit of wisdom each time you view your life from a macro-perspective—distancing yourself enough to see what is really going on, beyond the apparentness of the situation.

Finding the wisdom inside you and reaching your highest levels of evolution can be one of the most selfless lessons you can learn. It is the one that will elevate you and propel you along your own path so that you may contribute the results of all your other lessons to the rest of the world.

LIMITLESSNESS

"What we call results are beginnings."
Ralph Waldo Emerson

The final lesson you must learn as you embrace the Ten Rules for Being Human is limitlessness, for that will keep you traveling along your path long after you finish reading this book. Limitlessness is the sense that there are no boundaries to what you can become or do. You learn it when you know that your evolution is never-ending and your potential for growth reaches to infinity.

You were born knowing your limitlessness. As you grew and became socialized in this world, however, you might have come to believe that there are boundaries that prevent you from reaching the highest levels of spiritual, emotional, or mental evolution. However, boundaries exist only in your mind. When you are able to transcend them, you learn the lesson of limitlessness.

When I was young, I had a teacher who understood the importance of this lesson. She reminded us every day that we could do anything we set our minds to, no matter how impossible it might seem or how strong the opposition. It is my sincere hope that there is a teacher like Mrs. Carbone in every school around the world, so that our children can know the wonder and power they have within themselves and will strive to access it.

The reason there is no end to the levels you can reach is because you already have infinite potential within you. Your challenge in this lifetime is simply to uncover that potential by peeling back the layers and remembering this essential truth: there is nothing you cannot do, be, or have. All is within your reach. Know your limits, not so that you can honor them, but so that you can smash them to pieces and reach for magnificence.

There was a story in the news recently about a

man named Valdas Adamkus who proved to himself and to the world that there is nothing a person cannot do. Valdas immigrated to the United States from Lithuania and, after years of hard work, rose to become a highly decorated government official. He implemented a massive environmental cleanup plan for the Great Lakes and received the nation's highest honor for government officials from President Ronald Reagan. In 1991, Lithuania became free, and Valdas realized he wanted to go back and help his home country the same way he had helped America.

In 1998, at the age of seventy-one, when many people would be retiring, Valdas Adamkus became the president of Lithuania. When asked about his inner process that led him to run for such a demanding office at his age, Valdas replied, "There are no limits in life."

Countless others have shown us similar spirit, proving that a person can do whatever he or she strives to do. The Wright brothers created a machine that flies, despite the doubt that surrounded them. Gandhi inspired a revolution that affected millions of people.

Accomplishments need not be heroic to illustrate limitlessness. Whether it is getting an A on a term paper or putting up the kitchen curtains by yourself, you can prove to yourself that you can do anything at all even by executing the smallest actions.

What is important is that you believe that you can do it and that you give yourself every opportunity to succeed.

Each lesson you learn in your lifetime will open doorways to your own sense of limitlessness. There is no limit to your compassion or patience, nor to your willingness, commitment, tolerance, or any other pocket of understanding you reach into. You have infinite permission to love, to grow, and to re-remember all the wisdom within you.

SUMMARY

Your time here on Earth is brief. Time passes and things change. You have options and choices in which to make your wishes, dreams, and goals become reality.

When you ask yourself, "Why am I here?" or "Why is this happening to me?" or "What's it all about?" turn to your spiritual primer. Ask yourself, "What is the lesson?" If you hear a defensive reaction using the words "never" or "always" in your response, you haven't yet learned the lesson. Next, go a little deeper and ask, "What is there for me to learn from this experience?"

Each time you view your circumstances as possessing value, regardless of the apparent confusion or hardship, you grow. Your personal evolution will depend on how readily you embrace your lessons and integrate them into your life. Remember, the only consequence for resisting lessons, is that they will keep repeating themselves until you learn them. When you have learned a lesson, you will always be tested. When the lesson is learned, the test will be easily passed, and you then move on to more complex and challenging ones.

You can look back on the incidents in your past and see clearly the lessons you have learned, resisted, and are still repeating. "Yesterday is history, tomorrow is a mystery, and today is a gift, that is why we call it the present."

It is more challenging to look at your present situation and see exactly what your lessons are. Looking into the future is the most difficult. Wishing that you had already graduated from the school of life does not accelerate your progress or make the lessons any easier. Examining the situation for the real lesson is the scavenger hunt.

> Remind yourself that you are here to learn lessons.
> Be present with your process. Pay attention to what you are experiencing.
> Be diligent with actions which enable you to "get" the lessons presented to you.
> Ask for answers and you shall receive them.
> Listen with an open heart.
> Explore all options.
> See your judgment as a mirror.
> View each crisis as an opportunity.
> Trust yourself.
> Believe in yourself.

Look within yourself, to your higher self, for
  guidance on all your choices.
Extend compassion to yourself.
Remember, there are no mistakes, only lessons
  (Rule Three).
Love yourself, trust your choices, and
  everything is possible!

ABOUT THE AUTHOR

Dr. Chérie Carter-Scott is an entrepreneur, international lecturer, consultant, trainer, author, coach, seminar leader, and chairman of the board of the MMS (Motivation Management Service) Institute, Inc., which specializes in personal growth and professional training. She has worked with more than 200,000 people in workshops and private consultations all over the world, including corporate clients such as IBM, GTE, Burger King, and American Express. She lives in Santa Barbara with her husband, daughter, and sister.

She has twenty-five years experience as a speaker, management consultant, trainer, and teacher. She is the author of four books.

Dr. Carter-Scott received her Ph.D. in human and organizational development with an emphasis on the relationship between employee satisfaction and customer satisfaction and has designed twenty-three courses on Powerpoint for professional and personal growth. Dr. Carter-Scott's special gift is to ask the perfect question, enabling people to discover their own answers to their life lessons. She also helps turn negative attitudes into positive behaviors.

Dr. Carter-Scott is known for motivating individuals to take charge of their lives and to make the seemingly impossible happen. She is hired by Fortune 500 companies, associations, family-owned businesses, and entrepreneurs as a facilitator and "coach" and has been called a guardian angel to CEOs.

Dr. Carter-Scott has appeared on *Oprah*, *Regis & Kathie Lee*, CNN, and over 200 radio talk shows. She has presented her seminars, workshops, and keynote speeches in twelve countries on three continents and her tapes, speeches, and books have touched the lives of millions worldwide.

She is co-author of *Chicken Soup for the Global Soul* with Jack Canfield and Mark Victor Hansen, which is scheduled to be published in 2000.

The following opportunities are ways to participate with Dr. Carter-Scott and The MMS (Motivation Management Service) Institute, Inc.

- Participating in Personal Growth Programs or Professional Trainings such as:

    The Inner Negotiation Workshop

    Facilitator Training or Consultants Training

- Corporate Consultation or Trainings:

    Visioning

    Managing Change in Corporations

Team Building

- Management Development Courses including:
    Communication Skills
    Conflict Management
    Consultative Sales Training
    Customer Satisfaction
    How to Run Successful Meetings
    Interviewing Skills
    Performance Appraisal
    Presentation Skills
    Stress Management
    Time Management

- Booking Dr. Carter-Scott as a speaker for your group

- Ordering additional copies of: *If Life Is a Game, These Are the Rules*

- Purchasing other books and tapes by Dr. Chérie Carter-Scott:

    Negaholics: How to Overcome Negativity and Turn Your Life Around

    The Corporate Negaholic: How to Successfully Deal with Negative Colleagues, Managers, and Corporations

    The New Species: The Evolution of the Human Being

    The Inner View: A Woman's Daily Journal

- Being added to The MMS Institute's mailing
  list:

  Call: (800) 321-6342 (NEGA) or
  in California: (805) 563-0789
  visit our Web site: www.themms.com
  Fax: (805) 563-1028
  E-mail: 75507.3167@compuserve.com
  cherie@themms.com

Dear Reader,

If Life Is a Game, These Are the Rules: The Ten Rules for Being Human is about why we are on Earth. This work is about listening to, trusting, and honoring your inner knowing or voice. A cornerstone of the work is respect for each individual and his or her choices. Each person possesses the knowing as well as the personal power to make his or her dreams come true and fulfill his or her spiritual DNA or life's purpose.

I founded The MMS Institute, Inc. in 1974 to help people live according to the principles in this book.

If you are interested in continuing your spiritual path through any of the courses we offer through our global network, please contact us at our world headquarters in Santa Barbara to connect with our affiliates in Holland, Switzerland, Sweden, and elsewhere.

May you learn all the lessons on your path and make all of your dreams come true.

Chérie Carter-Scott, Ph.D.

Chérie Carter-Scott, Ph.D.